THE
INVISIBLE
KING
AND HIS
KINGDOM

THE
INVISIBLE
KING
AND HIS
KINGDOM

JOHN ECKHARDT

CHARISMA
HOUSE

Most CHARISMA HOUSE BOOK GROUP products are available at special quantity discounts for bulk purchase for sales promotions, premiums, fund-raising, and educational needs. For details, write Charisma House Book Group, 600 Rinehart Road, Lake Mary, Florida 32746, or telephone (407) 333-0600.

THE INVISIBLE KING AND HIS KINGDOM by John Eckhardt
Published by Charisma House
Charisma Media/Charisma House Book Group
600 Rinehart Road
Lake Mary, Florida 32746
www.charismahouse.com

Cover design by Justin Evans
Design Director: Bill Johnson

Visit the author's Web site at www.impactnetwork.net.

Library of Congress Cataloging-in-Publication Data:

Eckhardt, John, 1957-
  The invisible king and his kingdom / John Eckhardt. -- 1st ed.
    p. cm.
  Includes bibliographical references.
  ISBN 978-1-61638-279-7 (trade paper) -- ISBN 978-1-61638-420-3 (e-book)
1. Kingdom of God. 2. Jesus Christ--Royal office. 3. Jesus Christ--Kingdom. I. Title.
  BT94.E25 2011
  231.7'2--dc22

                              2011012744

First Edition

11 12 13 14 15 — 9 8 7 6 5 4 3 2 1
Printed in the United States of America

Contents

INTRODUCTION

THERE WERE MANY who heard the word of the kingdom and did not understand it. The kingdom was a mystery that was revealed to some and hidden from others. This book is designed to give you a greater understanding of the kingdom.

It is important to understand the kingdom in its first-century context. What would the announcement of the kingdom mean to a Jew living in the time of Christ? What is the historical context of the kingdom message? What forces were at work during the time of the announcement? This book will help you understand the context, and this will result in a much greater understanding of the kingdom of heaven.

The announcement of the kingdom does not arrive in a vacuum. There is a historical backdrop to the arrival of the kingdom. Jesus came in the fullness of time, at the end of the age (or consummation of the age). The time was set (fulfillment). It is impossible to understand kingdom without having a historical perspective. You cannot just pick up the Bible, go to Matthew's account, read it, and completely understand the message of the kingdom.

The kingdom of God is the rule of God over Israel and worldwide. The hope of Israel was the hope of a golden age of righteousness ushered in by the Messiah, the Son of David. They were looking for the restoration of the Davidic kingdom and the rebuilding of the tabernacle of David. The kingdom would be the age of the Messiah.

The Messiah would be a victorious king who would defeat Israel's enemies and rule in righteousness. This was the hope of the prophets. These prophecies were given in times of great apostasy and darkness. When Israel lived under the yoke of foreign enemies, they held on to these prophecies as hope for a bright future. During the darkest days and years of suffering and defeat, these prophecies gave them hope.

The prophets used figurative language to describe the kingdom age that was coming.

- The eyes of the blind would be opened and the ears of the deaf unstopped (Isa. 35:5).

- The lame man would leap as a deer, and the tongue of the dumb would sing. Waters would break out in the wilderness and streams in the desert (Isa. 35:6).

- A highway would be built called the way of holiness (Isa. 35:8).

- The ransomed of the Lord would return and come to Zion with songs and everlasting joy (Isa. 35:10).

- Zion would be comforted and her warfare accomplished (Isa. 40:1–2).

- The glory of the Lord would be revealed, and all flesh would see it together (Isa. 40:5).

- The Lord would come with a strong hand and rule and feed His flock like a shepherd and gather the lambs with His arms (Isa. 40:10–11).

The Servant of the Lord would bring judgment to the nations and would set judgment in the earth. He would be given as a covenant to the people and a light to the Gentiles. He would open the eyes of the blind and bring the prisoners out of the prison house (Isa. 61:1). People would declare His praise in the islands. He would make darkness light and crooked things straight (Isa. 42:12, 16).

The Lord would pour water upon the thirsty and floods upon the dry ground. He would pour His spirit upon Israel's seed and blessing upon their offspring. He would blot out their transgressions and sins and redeem them (Isa. 44).

The Lord would raise up the tribes of Israel and restore the preserved of Israel. He would be a light to the Gentiles and salvation to the ends of the earth. He would hear in the acceptable time and help in the day of salvation. He would establish the earth and cause them to inherit the desolate heritages. They would no longer hunger or thirst; neither would the sun smite them. He would have mercy on them and guide them by springs of water. He would make the mountains a way, and His highways would be exalted. The heavens would sing; the earth would be joyful; the mountains would break forth into singing because of the Lord's comfort and mercy. The Gentiles would bring their sons in their arms and their daughters upon their shoulders. Kings would be their nursing fathers and queens their nursing mothers. All flesh would know that the Lord was their Savior and Redeemer (Isa. 49).

The Lord would comfort Zion and comfort her waste places and make her wilderness like Eden and her desert like the garden of the Lord. Righteousness and salvation would come. The heavens would vanish away like smoke and the earth wax old like a garment, but His salvation would be forever—and salvation from generation to generation (Isa. 51:6, 8).

Glad tidings will come; salvation would be published. The waste places of Zion would break forth in joy and sing together. The Lord would make bare His holy arm in the eyes of the nations, and the ends of the earth would see the salvation of God. Many nations would be sprinkled, and kings would shut their mouth at the Messiah (Isa. 52:15).

The barren would break forth into singing and need to enlarge the place of her tent, for it would break forth on the left hand and on the right hand. God would be called "the God of the earth." God's covenant of peace would not be removed. God would lay her stones with fair colors and her foundations with sapphires. Israel's children would be taught of the Lord and would have great peace (Isa. 54).

Nations would run to Israel because of God's glory. They would go out with joy and be led forth with peace. The mountains and hills would break forth into singing, and the trees of the field would clap their hands. Instead of the thorn tree, the fir tree would come up, and instead of the brier shall come up the myrtle tree (Isa. 55:12–13).

God would bring the sons of the stranger to His holy mountain and make them joyful in the house of prayer. Their offerings would be accepted, and God's house would be a house of prayer for all nations. God would gather the outcasts of Israel and others to Him (Isa. 56:7–8).

The Lord would come and repay fury to His adversaries and recompense to His enemies. The Redeemer would come to Zion and turn transgression from Jacob. The Spirit and the Word would not depart from their seed, or their seed's seed, forever (Isa. 59:21).

- The lion and lamb would lie together.

- The mountains would drop wine and milk.

- The Spirit would be poured from on high.

- There would be showers of blessings.

- A new covenant would come.

- The desert place would bloom, and the dry ground would receive water.

- The owl and dragons would be satisfied.

- A new people would be created to praise the Lord.

- Jerusalem would be created a joy and a rejoicing.

- Strangers would be joined to Israel.

- God would pour out His Spirit upon their seed.

- The nations would come bowing and bringing gifts.

- A highway of holiness would be built.

- The redeemed of the Lord would come to Zion with singing, and everlasting joy would be upon their heads.

- Israel would be redeemed.

- Healing would come.

- The ruins would be rebuilt.

- The desolate places would be restored.

- A king would reign in righteousness and justice.

- The king would smite the nations with a rod of iron.

- Prosperity would come.

- Mountains would be made low and valleys exalted.

- The meek would inherit the earth.

- Deliverance and salvation would come.

- Peace (*shalom* in Hebrew) would flow like a river.

- The wicked would be judged.

- Praise and worship would spring from the nations.

- The day of the Lord would arrive.

- The Sun of righteousness would come with healing in His wings.

- The river of God would flow from the temple, bringing healing to the nations.

- Their seed would inherit the nations.

- They would be trees of righteousness, the planting of the Lord.

- They would be priests and ministers of God.

- The day of salvation would come.

Salvation, redemption, praise, worship, righteousness, justice, holiness, singing, joy, rejoicing, healing, restoration, prosperity, peace, abundance, safety, protection, blessing, life, reconciliation, newness, and favor would come.

Jesus came to announce the year of the Lord's favor, or the year of jubilee (Luke 4:18–19; Lev. 25:8–25). In the year of jubilee, land is restored, debts are canceled, and slaves are released. The kingdom is our *jubilee*. When you come into the kingdom, you enter into rest and receive *favor*.

As a result of the kingdom, shame, ruin, confusion, sickness, death, poverty, bondage, oppression, sadness, defeat, humiliation, sin, iniquity, cursing, fear, lack, and barrenness would be banished.

The kingdom would be a time of salvation and deliverance. The kingdom would be a new era of salvation history, with multitudes being saved from generation to generation.

The announcement of the kingdom was an announcement that what Israel had been waiting for was now at hand. The hope of previous generations had arrived. The time had finally come. After years of defeat and shame, salvation was at hand. The Messiah (Deliverer) was at hand. No wonder it is called good news and glad tidings. Those who heard it received the word of the kingdom with JOY.

The announcement of the kingdom was the announcement of all the hopes of Israel. It was an announcement that the prophetic words were about to be fulfilled. Many had probably given up hope after so many years of failure. Some probably no longer believed. But there was always a remnant in Israel who remained faithful to the covenant and kept the hope of their fathers. They believed that these promises were true and continued to believe in them. Some may have mocked, but others remained convinced they were at hand. Some, like Anna and Simeon, knew the day was at hand. They prayed and fasted for the kingdom to arrive.

The Jews were living under the iron hand of the Romans when this message came. Most of the people in the land were living in poverty and ignorance. Israel was living under the heavy taxation of the Romans. Jesus came preaching this message to the poor. The poor, the oppressed, the sick, and the demonized heard this message of the kingdom. It was their only hope of escaping a miserable situation.

The subject of the kingdom of God is not about the overall reign of God throughout history. God has always been sovereign. The message of the kingdom is about His redemptive reign, His salvific reign. The message of Christ was that the kingdom was "at hand." There was an aspect of His reign that was arriving. This means it had not yet arrived.

Everlasting righteousness, eternal redemption, reconciliation, and remission of sins were at hand. This could only be accomplished through the blood of the Lamb of God and through faith in His blood. This is what Daniel saw in his vision of the seventy weeks.

The rule of Christ would be His rule through salvation. This salvation would be the work of Christ through His death and resurrection. It would be His rule through the operation of the Holy Spirit. Christ would rule in the hearts of His saints. The rule would be spiritual, not earthly or physical. The redemption prophesied by the prophets was at hand.

The kingdom of God announced is the announcement of a new era, a new age. Light and glory were arriving. Salvation and deliverance had come. Judgment had arrived. Things were about to be set straight. Mountains were about to be made low, and valleys were about to be exalted. The wicked were about to be judged and the righteous rewarded. This was the turning point in human history. This was the consummation of the ages.

The Hope of Israel had arrived. The expectation of the nation was at its highest. For many, this hope would be seemingly dashed. A week after Christ's triumphant entry, He would be crucified. Was this God's plan? Yes, it was. Isaiah prophesied the Messiah's death. Daniel spoke of Him being cut off. Jesus continually spoke of His rejection and death.

In this book you will learn that the kingdom of God is invisible and does not come with observation. The kingdom is the rule of God through Christ over His new-creation people, the church. It is the rule of God over Zion, the mountain of the Lord. It is the rule of the Good Shepherd over His flock. It is the inward rule of God in the hearts of His saints. It is the rule of God through the Holy Spirit. It is the rule of God through the new covenant.

You will learn that the kingdom of God and the kingdom of heaven are two descriptions of the same kingdom. The kingdom is God's rule, and it is from heaven. Heaven is the origin of the kingdom, not earth.

The church is not an alternate plan. The church has always been the plan of God. The church is not a parenthesis. Jesus began to speak of the church to His disciples. The church would be the people over whom the gates of hell would not be able to prevail.

The church is the *ekklesia*. The church consists of the called-out ones. The called are those who rule and reign with Christ. The church is the embassy of Christ. The church consists of kingdom citizens born from above. The church consists of people from every nation who are submitted to the rule of Christ through the Holy Spirit. They are the ones who call Jesus, Lord.

The kingdom is not earthly and geographical. Geography does not determine where the kingdom exists. The kingdom is determined by its citizens no matter where they live geographically.

King David's earthly reign was limited to a physical, geographical area. The land of Canaan was a type of the world. Israel's physical land was a picture of the earth. Israel was a microcosm of a global kingdom. The land belonged to God, but the earth is the Lord's. Christ's kingdom cannot be limited to a geographical location. The earthly type was only a picture of the universal, spiritual kingdom that was coming. Types, antitypes, signs, and shadows are absolutely indispensable for proper scriptural interpretation. (A *type* is a biblical person, thing, action, event, ceremony, structure, furniture, color, or number that prefigures an *antitype* of the same in the New Testament.) The antitype of the New Testament is vastly superior to its type in the Old Testament:

- David and Solomon were types of Christ and His kingdom.

- Hezekiah and Josiah were types of Christ and His kingdom, restoration.

- Moses was a type of Christ, the Deliverer and Lawgiver.

- Joshua was a type of Christ and His kingdom.

- Sarah was a type of the church, the free woman, the kingdom.

- Earthly Zion was a type of heavenly Zion.

- Earthly Jerusalem was a type of the new Jerusalem.

- The earthly temple was a type of the spiritual temple (the church).

- The land of Israel was a type of the world.

- The sabbath day was a type of the rest of Christ and the kingdom.

- The year of jubilee was a type of the kingdom.

- Tabernacles were a type of the gathering of the nations, the kingdom.

- The tabernacle of David was a type of the kingdom.

In order to be instructed in the kingdom, you must be able to bring forth truth from the old and new covenants. The old was a type and symbol of the new. Earthly Jerusalem was a type of the heavenly Jerusalem. The earthly temple was a type of the church, the spiritual temple. Earthly Zion was a type of heavenly Zion. David's earthly rule was a type of the heavenly rule of Christ. The failure to understand the type and the antitype is a major reason why some fail to understand the kingdom.

It is also important to understand that the kingdom cannot be tied to any one geographical place. The church began in Jerusalem, but eventually Jerusalem was destroyed. There have been many moves of

God throughout history. Some places that have had great revivals are no longer experiencing revival. The move of God has always shifted from place to place. The kingdom is fluid. The kingdom moves wherever people are hungry and submitted to the Holy Spirit.

Regardless of how it looks, the kingdom is always advancing. The kingdom of God is always at work, even when we do not perceive it to be so. Some parts of the world are experiencing tremendous revival, while others are spiritually stagnant. The kingdom is always growing. The rule of Christ continues to advance from generation to generation. This is the prophetic promise of Isaiah: "of the increase of His government and peace there shall be no end" (Isa. 9:7). The church has grown from 120 on the Day of Pentecost in Jerusalem to a global company of millions.

The preaching of the kingdom did not begin with the church but with John and Jesus. The church, however, was established as a result of the kingdom message. The kingdom was prophesied by the prophets and came into fulfillment at the coming of Christ.

You will learn that the rule of God over His church brings peace and prosperity. God brings us to His holy mountain and plants us in Zion. The Lord has brought us to His high place, His holy hill, where we are taught truth and righteousness.

You will learn that the kingdom is eternal and has no end. The kingdom will increase from generation to generation. The kingdom is global and not limited to a certain geographical location.

You will learn that the kingdom is the place of God's glory, salvation, healing, and redemption. It is a place of liberty and freedom.

You will learn that the kingdom is filled with people of praise and worship. Zion is a place of dancing, rejoicing, shouting, and music.

God's promise to Abraham is the foundation of the kingdom. The kingdom brings blessing to all families of the earth.

> Now the LORD had said unto Abram, Get thee out of thy
> country, and from thy kindred, and from thy father's
> house, unto a land that I will shew thee: And I will make
> of thee a great nation, and I will bless thee, and make thy
> name great; and thou shalt be a blessing: And I will bless
> them that bless thee, and curse him that curseth thee:
> and in thee shall all families of the earth be blessed.
> —GENESIS 12:1–3, KJV

Through the Messiah all the families of the earth are blessed.
The kingdom is Christ's salvific rule over the nations. The blessing of
salvation is for all the families of the earth.

> Then said he unto them, Therefore every scribe which
> is instructed unto the kingdom of heaven is like unto a
> man that is an householder, which bringeth forth out of
> his treasure things new and old.
> —MATTHEW 13:52, KJV

The kingdom of God has been forcefully advancing since the days
of John the Baptist. It is still advancing today. The New International
Version renders Matthew 11:12 as, "The kingdom of heaven has been
forcefully advancing, and forceful men lay hold of it."

John preached as the forerunner, in a sense as the last sentinel
of the night, proclaiming the dawn of a new day. Jesus was Himself
the light; He brought the day into existence. The arrival of the
kingdom was the arrival of the *day*. The *night* was ending. Sorrow,
spiritual death, and pain were ending, and salvation, life, and joy
were arriving.

> And there shall be no night there; and they need no
> candle, neither light of the sun; for the Lord God giveth
> them light: and they shall reign for ever and ever.
> —REVELATION 22:5, KJV

The reign of God is connected to the end of the night. There is no night in Zion. The Lord is our light. We live in the glorious light of the kingdom. Hallelujah!

CHAPTER 1

A KINGDOM WITHOUT OBSERVATION

JESUS DID NOT submit to Israel's desire for an earthly king. He told the Jewish leaders that His kingdom does not come with observation.

> Now when He was asked by the Pharisees when the kingdom of God would come, He answered them and said, "The kingdom of God does not come with observation."
>
> —LUKE 17:20

The Pharisees were looking for an observable kingdom. These Pharisees expected a visible, temporal kingdom. They were looking for a worldly kingdom. They could not understand the nature of the kingdom that Jesus preached. They were carnal and earthly; Jesus was spiritual and heavenly.

The kingdom was in their midst, and they could not discern it. Healing and deliverance were signs that the kingdom had come nigh.

The reason mortal man finds it difficult to absorb this subject is because of the limited perception we have for the world of the unseen. The world of the unseen is a spiritual dimension, and we have only the five senses of human nature (seeing, hearing, feeling, smelling, and tasting). These senses are the physiological methods of perception. The word *perception* is derived from the Latin words *perceptio* and *percipio* and means "receiving, collecting; action of taking possession; apprehension with the mind or senses."[1]

Jesus understood this human limitation when He walked on Earth. When Nicodemus asked Jesus to explain the kingdom of God, Jesus replied, "If I tell you things that are plain as the hand before your face and you don't believe me, what use is there in telling you of things you can't see, the things of God?" (John 3:12, THE MESSAGE). Later, when He was speaking to the disciples about His imminent departure from them, He said to them, "You are from beneath; I am from above. You are of this world; I am not of this world" (John 8:23).

When Jesus stood before Pilate after the Pharisees captured Him, and Pilate asked Him if He was indeed the king of the Jews, Jesus replied, "My kingdom is not of this world. If My kingdom were of this world, My servants would fight, so that I should not be delivered to the Jews; but now My kingdom is not from here" (John 18:36).

Jesus did not come to Earth to establish a worldly kingdom. The kingdom would not be established in a worldly way. There would be no earthly armies needed. The kingdom would be advanced through the preaching of the gospel.

There were some in Israel who believed in bringing in the kingdom of God by force. They were called zealots. They hated the Romans and the fact that the covenant people lived under Gentile rule. Many of them believed in taking up arms against the Romans. They believed that when the Messiah came, He would do the same. Some believed they could hasten and force the coming of Messiah through armed rebellion.

But the kingdom would not come this way.

THE KINGDOM OF GOD— EARTHLY OR HEAVENLY?

The kingdom of God came to Earth through the suffering and death of the Christ. Most in Israel did not understand this, even though it had been spoken of by the prophets. How could a suffering Messiah bring the kingdom? Suffering and death were pictures of defeat, not victory.

They were looking for an earthly kingdom. They did not understand the kingdom or the prophets. The carnal mind cannot comprehend the things of the spirit. Earthly people understand earthly kingdoms. Earthly kingdoms are advanced through earthly means, usually warfare and bloodshed. Jesus preached about the kingdom of heaven. The kingdom of God is a heavenly kingdom.

The kingdom they were looking for did not arrive. For a generation after Jesus's death and resurrection, nothing changed; the Romans were still in control. What had happened? At the end of that generation, the Romans came in force and destroyed the city and the temple. Thousands of Jews perished, and thousands more were scattered to the nations. What happened to the kingdom? What happened to the hope? There was no earthly messiah sitting on the throne in Jerusalem. Jerusalem had become a burning heap. The Romans were victors, and the Jews were defeated.

Was Jesus just another false messiah? Was He just another deceiver? Was His announcement of the kingdom a lie? Did He give false hope to Israel? There certainly was no earthly kingdom. There certainly was no earthly throne. There certainly was no physical deliverance.

Could they have misinterpreted the message of the kingdom? Did they misunderstand the prophecies of the prophets? Was the message of the kingdom hidden from their eyes?

This is exactly what Jesus taught; He taught that the kingdom was *a mystery*. It was hidden from the eyes of the disobedient and rebellious and was revealed only to the humble. Many could not see the kingdom and would not be allowed to enter into it. The kingdom would not be given to a rebellious people. It was not an earthly kingdom and would never be apprehended by earthly people. The door would be shut to them but opened to those who humbled themselves and believed the gospel.

Entrance into the kingdom would not be determined by physical birth. Physical birth was very important to the Jews. Abraham is the first person in the Bible identified as a *Hebrew*. Paul identified himself as a "Hebrew of the Hebrews" (Phil. 3:5). The Jews considered themselves the descendants of Abraham and therefore the elect of God. Many depended on their physical descent rather than on faith in God.

Although Abraham was called a Hebrew, he was a Hittite. There were also Gentiles in the genealogy of Christ (Rahab and Ruth, Matt. 1:5), which shows that God always honored faith. To replace faith with physical descent was pride and abominable to God. God's choice of Israel had nothing to do with them; He chose Israel because of the covenant He made with Abraham. (See Deuteronomy 7:6–8.)

The proud would not enter the kingdom.

The rebellious would not enter the kingdom.

The immoral would not enter the kingdom.

Only a remnant would enter the kingdom, and the rest would be judged.

Worldly kingdoms are full of earthly pomp. They are defended by armies engaged in war. In *Barnes' Notes on the New Testament* we read:

> The charge on which Jesus was arraigned was that of laying claim to the office of a king. He here substantially admits that he *did* claim to be a king, but not in the sense in which the Jews understood it. They charged him with attempting to set up an *earthly* kingdom, and of exciting sedition against Caesar. In reply to this, Jesus says that *his kingdom is not of this world*. That is, it is not of the same nature as earthly kingdoms. It was not originated for the same purpose, or conducted on the same plan. He immediately adds a circumstance in which they differ. The kingdoms of the world are defended by arms; they maintain armies and engage in wars. If the kingdom of Jesus had been of *this* kind, he would have excited the multitudes that followed him to prepare for battle. He would have armed the hosts that attended him to Jerusalem. He would not have been alone and unarmed in the garden of Gethsemane. But though he *was* a king, yet his dominion was over the heart, subduing evil passions and corrupt desires, and bringing the soul to the love of peace and unity.[2]

Jesus never took upon Himself any earthly power. He did not raise up an army to gain control of an earthly kingdom. Matthew Henry gives the following account of Christ's introduction of the kingdom of God to His followers:

> He never took upon him any earthly power, never were any traitorous principles or practices laid to him. Christ gave an account of the nature of his kingdom. Its nature is not worldly; it is a kingdom within men, set

up in their hearts and consciences; its riches spiritual, its power spiritual, and it glory within. Its supports are not worldly; its weapons are spiritual; it needed not, nor used, force to maintain and advance it, nor opposed any kingdom but that of sin and Satan. Its object and design are not worldly.[3]

The earthly city of Jerusalem was a type of the heavenly Jerusalem. Jesus wept over the city because the people of Jerusalem missed the time of their visitation. Jesus did not establish an earthly kingdom there but instead pronounced judgment upon the city. The earthly hopes of many in Israel were dashed to pieces. Their hope of a glorious, earthly kingdom, headquartered in Jerusalem, did not come to pass.

The prophet Daniel saw the rise and fall of earthly kingdoms before the arrival of God's kingdom. He saw the kingdoms of Babylon, Persia, Greece, and Rome being replaced and falling. The kingdom would come and be an everlasting kingdom that filled the earth.

> You watched while a stone was cut out without hands, which struck the image on its feet of iron and clay, and broke them in pieces. Then the iron, the clay, the bronze, the silver, and the gold were crushed together, and became like chaff from the summer threshing floors; the wind carried them away so that no trace of them was found. And the stone that struck the image became a great mountain and filled the whole earth.
> —DANIEL 2:34–35

Notice that the stone becomes a mountain that fills the earth. The mountain is Zion, and Zion fills the earth. This is because Zion is a people and no longer a geographical location.

The kingdom is not earthly but is cut out without hands. There were many who heard about the kingdom but did not understand it. They were looking for the earthly and could not see the heavenly. Jesus spoke of these people when He said, "When anyone hears the word of the kingdom, and does not understand it, then the wicked one comes and snatches away what was sown in his heart. This is he who received seed by the wayside" (Matt. 13:19). They were looking for the earthly and could not see the heavenly.

It was hidden from the eyes of many in fulfillment of Isaiah's 23 prophecy.

> So when they had appointed him a day, many came to him at his lodging, to whom he explained and solemnly testified of the kingdom of God, persuading them concerning Jesus from both the Law of Moses and the Prophets, from morning till evening. And some were persuaded by the things which were spoken, and some disbelieved. So when they did not agree among themselves, they departed after Paul had said one word: "The Holy Spirit spoke rightly through Isaiah the prophet to our fathers, saying, "Go to this people and say: 'Hearing you will hear, and shall not understand; and seeing you will see, and not perceive; for the hearts of this people have grown dull. Their ears are hard of hearing, and their eyes they have closed, lest they should see with their eyes and hear with their ears, lest they should understand with their hearts and turn, so that I should heal them.'"
>
> —ACTS 28:23–27

HEAVENLY ZION

The revelation of heavenly Zion, the heavenly Jerusalem, is one of the most important for us to take a look at if we are going to understand

21

the kingdom. God rules over heavenly Zion. We have come to the heavenly city, not the earthly (Heb. 12:22). Our citizenship is in heaven. We are born from above, from the heavenly city, by spiritual birth. This is the place of the rule of God, the place of the kingdom. God's rule is over Zion, the heavenly people, the church.

In his commentary, Adam Clarke makes several important observations about the text of Hebrews 12:22:

> [But ye are come unto mount Sion] In order to enter fully into the apostle's meaning, we must observe,
>
> 1. That the Church, which is called here the city of the living God, the heavenly Jerusalem, and mount Sion, is represented under the notion of a city.
>
> 2. That the great assembly of believers in Christ is here opposed to the congregation of the Israelites assembled at Mount Sinai.
>
> 3. That the innumerable company of angels is here opposed to, those angels by whom the law was ushered in, Acts 7:53; Gal. 3:19.
>
> 4. That the Gospel first-born, whose names are written in heaven, are here opposed to the enrolled first-born among the Israelites, Ex. 24:5; 19:22.
>
> 5. That the mediator of the new covenant, the Lord Jesus, is here opposed to Moses, the mediator of the old.
>
> 6. And that the blood of sprinkling, of Christ, our High Priest, refers to the act of Moses, Ex. 24:8: "And Moses took the blood, and sprinkled it on the people, and said, Behold the blood of the covenant, which the Lord hath made with you concerning all these words."

[The heavenly Jerusalem] This phrase means the Church of the New Testament, as Schoettgen has amply proved in his dissertation on this subject.

[To an innumerable company of angels] To myriads, tens of thousands, of angels. These are represented as the attendants upon God, when he manifests himself in any external manner to mankind. When he gave the law at Mount Sinai, it is intimated that myriads of these holy beings attended him. "The chariots of the Lord are twenty thousand, even thousands of angels; the Lord is among them as in Sinai, in the holy place;" Ps. 68:17. And when he shall come to judge the world, he will be attended with a similar company. "Thousand thousands ministered unto him, and ten thousand times ten thousand stood before him;" Dan. 7:10. In both these cases, as in several others, these seem to be, speaking after the manner of men, the body guard of the Almighty. Though angels make a part of the inhabitants of the New Jerusalem, yet they belong also to the church below. Christ has in some sort incorporated them with his followers, for "they are all ministering spirits, sent forth to minister to them that shall be heirs of salvation," and they are all ever considered as making a part of God's subjects.[4]

God brought Israel out of Egypt through the wilderness into the land of Canaan. He planted them in the mountain, earthly Jerusalem, earthly Zion. This was a type of the heavenly. God now brings us into His mountain, heavenly Jerusalem, heavenly Zion. The Lord will reign forever and ever. This is the eternal kingdom, connected to the eternal city, heavenly Zion.

Zion is the mountain of God. The Lord's house was established at the top of the mountain (Isa. 2:2). The Lord's house, the church, is where we come to learn the ways of the Lord and be taught. It is a place of teaching. In speaking of the future house of God, Isaiah the prophet said:

> "Come, and let us go up to the mountain of the LORD, to the house of the God of Jacob; He will teach us His ways, and we shall walk in His paths." For out of Zion shall go forth the law, and the word of the LORD from Jerusalem.
>
> —ISAIAH 2:3

The word of the Lord comes through the church, the mountain of the Lord's house. Zion is a mountain that has an ensign to which the nations gather. The nations come to be taught the ways of God. The word of the Lord came from Jerusalem. The church began in Jerusalem. The apostles taught from Jerusalem. Zion began in Jerusalem and spread throughout the earth.

Those who put their trust in the Lord inherit the holy mountain. Those who believe the gospel are those who put their trust in Him. We come to Zion, the mountain of God, the place of God's rule, by faith. There were many who did not put their trust in the Lord but put their trust in the Law and in their good works. They did not trust in the grace of God and did not inherit the holy mountain.

Those who put their trust in the Lord and believed the gospel were brought by God to the holy mountain. We come to this mountain by faith. Zion, the mountain of God, the place of God's rule, is also the place of prayer (Isa. 56:7). The earthly house (temple) was no longer a place of prayer but a den of thieves. God created a new house of prayer, the church. In Acts 4:24 we read, "So when they heard that, they raised their voice to God with one accord and said: 'Lord, You are God, who made heaven and earth and the sea, and all that is in them.'"

God's rule is over Zion. Zion is a people. Zion is the dwelling place of God (Ps. 76:2). We are now God's dwelling place through the Spirit.

Jesus is the foundation of Zion, the church, the new creation. The foundation for earthly Jerusalem was in the mountains. The foundation for heavenly Zion is in Christ.

EARTHLY ZION VS. HEAVENLY ZION

The revelation of Zion is one of the most important in the Word of God. There was an earthly Zion, and there is a heavenly Zion. The earthly was a type of the heavenly. The heavenly is greater and is the reality of which the earthly was simply a symbol. One day heavenly Zion will cover the earth with the rule and reign of our invisible King. God reigns in Zion. When His rule and reign are established over all the earth, each of the following characteristics will be a part of His kingdom in Zion:

- Glory

- Salvation

- Righteousness

- Praise and worship

- Dominion and power

- The knowledge of God

- Deliverance

- Blessing

- The prophetic

- Elders (the apostolic) as part of the government

- The government of our King, Christ Jesus

Earthly Zion was the holy place, the place chosen by God. This was often emphasized by the psalms, because there were other *holy* places set up for worship that were not chosen by God. Jeroboam set up holy places in Bethel and Dan. The Samaritans worshiped in Mount Gerizim. These rival holy places were not legitimate. Zion was the only place chosen by God as His resting place.

The following factors about Zion demonstrate its importance above any illegitimate holy places:

- The Lord loves Zion more than any other place (Ps. 87:2).

- The Lord chose Zion for His habitation (Ps. 132:13).

- Zion is the joy of the whole earth (Ps. 48:2).

- Zion is the perfection of beauty from which God shines (Ps. 50:2).

- The tribe of Judah was chosen by God because He loves it (Ps. 78:68).

Earthly Zion as a type of heavenly Zion was limited to earthly Jerusalem. Heavenly Zion will be global and will cover the earth (Ps. 47:2, 7). All the earth will worship our invisible King, the Lord God (Ps. 66:4).

In Romans 10:18, Paul quotes from Psalm 19 in the context of the gospel, stating the prophetic words of verse 4: "Their sound has gone out to all the earth, and their words to the ends of the world." The gospel has gone out to all the earth, and people have responded with salvation and praise. In his commentary on Psalm 19:1–7, Matthew Henry adds this:

> The sun in the firmament is an emblem of the Sun of righteousness, the Bridegroom of the church, and the

Light of the world, diffusing divine light and salvation by his gospel to the nations of the earth. He delights to bless his church, which he has espoused to himself; and his course will be unwearied as that of the sun, till the whole earth is filled with his light and salvation.[5]

The kingdom of God is advanced through the preaching of the gospel. Those who hear and believe are brought to Zion, the mountain of God, the place of salvation, praise, worship, teaching, and glory. They come into the kingdom, the place of God's rule, Zion. They come to the ensign, the banner of the Lord, and submit to His rule.

> Sing praises to the LORD, who dwells in Zion!
> Declare His deeds among the people.
> —PSALM 9:11

This praise will someday be worldwide and not limited to an earthly place. What happened in earthly Zion was only a type of what is now happening around the globe.

> The earth is the LORD's, and all its fullness.
> —PSALM 24:1

God's ownership is not limited to a place in Palestine but is global. This is fulfilled in the church.

Zion is the stronghold of God. Zion was the city of David. It was a type of the city of the greater David, Jesus the Son of David. It is the joy of the whole earth. It is the city of the great King.

As the people of God, we are the redeemed, a holy people who dwell in a city set on a hill that is not forsaken (Isa. 62:12). We are a city set on a hill. We are the redeemed, the holy people, a city not forsaken.

The uncircumcised cannot be a part of this city. Only the circumcised and clean can be a part of this city (Isa. 52:1). We are circumcised with the circumcision of Christ, in the heart and not in the flesh. We can enter Zion because of this circumcision. We are cleansed through the blood of Christ and by walking in His light (1 John 1:7). The Lord rules over a holy people.

Zion is a chosen place and a chosen people. Zion is the habitation of God. We are chosen in Christ, and we are the habitation of God through the Spirit. God inhabits our praise.

THE PEOPLE OF ZION

When we have accepted the redemption of Christ, we are no longer strangers but have become fellow citizens with the saints of the household of God (Eph. 2:19). We have a right to enter and abide in the city.

This is the kingdom, the eternal reign of God (Ps. 146:10). Zion is the habitation of God through all generations. Zion exists from generation to generation, just as the kingdom exists from generation to generation. The saints speak of the glory of the kingdom from generation to generation.

> All Your works shall praise You, O Lord,
> And Your saints shall bless You.
> They shall speak of the glory of Your kingdom,
> And talk of Your power,
> To make known to the sons of men His mighty acts,
> And the glorious majesty of His kingdom.
> Your kingdom is an everlasting kingdom,
> And Your dominion endures throughout all generations.
> —Psalm 145:10–13

Every generation of the church praises God for His salvation and mighty acts. Like Zion and the kingdom, the church exists from generation to generation (Eph. 3:21). Isaiah 9:7 confirms: "Of the increase of His government [dominion] and peace there will be no end."

Jesus is the foundation of the new-covenant people, Zion. We are Zion; we are the place of God's rule. Old Testament prophecies are filled with expressions of the glories of our heavenly Zion. It is truly a glorious dwelling, and it will cause the saints to sing praises to our King continually and to declare His works to all people (Ps. 9:11).

Unlike the biblical kingdoms of Israel, or even our modern-day earthly kingdoms, the kingdom is filled with joy and peace. There will be no reason for any weeping, and the moment we cry to the Lord, He will hear and answer us (Isa. 30:19). He will put His own words in our mouths and will cover us in the shadow and protection of His own hand (Isa. 51:16).

What a transformation for the children of God. Chosen and loved by God, the Israelites were brought out of Egypt by the blood of a lamb and delivered from Pharaoh through the sea and the cloud. Though they wandered for forty long years in the wilderness, God brought them finally to the Promised Land and established Jerusalem as the city of God. But that was only a type of His marvelous future for the people of God. Just so, the people of God—Jew and Gentile alike—have been delivered out of the bondage of a spiritual Egypt by the blood of the Lamb of God. We have been cleansed by the living water of the new birth and led to our heavenly Zion by the cloud of God's Holy Spirit. We have entered the kingdom of God—heavenly Zion on the mountain of God. This is our journey to Zion.

Many people are looking for Zion. In Jeremiah 50:5 we read, "They shall ask the way to Zion, with their faces toward it, saying,

'Come and let us join ourselves to the LORD in a perpetual covenant that will not be forgotten.'" Can you direct them there?

A mountain is a symbol of power and strength. A mountain is an elevation, a high place. It is a place of safety, security, a place easily defended. In Zion we are protected from the enemy. Heavenly Zion cannot be invaded, conquered, or defeated. Isaiah 33:15–16 says, "He who walks righteously and speaks uprightly…will dwell on high; His place of defense will be the fortress of rocks; bread will be given him, his water will be sure." The King Himself ensures our eternal defense.

Whoever holds the high place has power and authority. Mountains represent kingdoms, or strong, powerful governments. The mountain of Zion is symbolic of the kingdom, the powerful government of God. When you come to Zion, you come into contact with the authority and power of God. The kingdom is the government of God, and the mountain is symbolic of that government. Those who come to Zion submit to the King.

Those who hate Zion cannot prosper. The enemies of the kingdom will be put to shame and turned back (Ps. 129:5). The kingdom and Zion were established in spite of the opposition of kings of the earth. Psalm 2 says that "the nations rage" and "the rulers take counsel together, against the LORD and against His Anointed," but "He who sits in the heavens shall laugh; the LORD shall hold them in derision. Then He shall speak to them in His wrath…'Yet I have set My King on My holy hill of Zion'" (vv. 1–2, 4–6). The psalmist ends the psalm with this good advice: "Now therefore, be wise, O kings…Blessed are all those who put their trust in Him" (vv. 10, 12).

THE ENEMIES OF THE KINGDOM

There were enemies of the earthly kingdom. David experienced much opposition on his way to the throne. David's sufferings foreshadowed the sufferings of Christ. The Spirit of Christ used David's sufferings to speak prophetically through him concerning the future enemies of Christ and His kingdom. God used David's prophetic judgments to decree judgment against the enemies of Christ. These are called *imprecatory psalms.* These psalms have been misunderstand and somewhat controversial; however, they must be understood in a kingdom context.

The imprecatory psalms contain serious words against the enemies of the kingdom. *Theopedia,* an encyclopedia of biblical Christianity available online, gives the following information about the imprecatory psalms.

> [The imprecatory psalms] contain curses or prayers for the punishment of the psalmist's enemies. To *imprecate* means "to invoke evil upon, or curse." Psalms 7, 35, 55, 58, 59, 69, 79, 109, 137 and 139 all contain prayers for God's judgment on the psalmist's enemies. Example imprecatory statements from the Psalms follow:
>
> Psalm 55:15—Let death take my enemies by surprise; let them go down alive to the grave.
>
> Psalm 56:6—O God, break the teeth in their mouths.
>
> Psalm 69:28—May they be blotted out of the book of life and not be listed with the righteous.
>
> Psalm 109:9—May his children be fatherless and his wife a widow.
>
> Psalm 137:9—How blessed will be the one who seizes your infants, and dashes them against the rocks.[6]

Theopedia clarifies that these psalms were not a matter of personal revenge. The writer did not have a personal vendetta against his enemy. Instead they were "utterances of zeal for the kingdom of God and his glory. To be sure, the attacks which provoked these prayers were not from personal enemies; rather, they were rightfully seen as attacks against God and especially his representatives in the promised line of the Messiah."[7]

There was a level of wickedness in those upon whom these imprecations fell. They were the enemies of the kingdom and were used by Satan to attempt to stop the kingdom from being established. These enemies were unaware of what they were up against. They were up against prophetic utterances that had been uttered through David and others. The enemies of Christ were destroyed, and His kingdom was established.

The imprecatory psalms contain curses upon those who fought against the promised line of the Messiah, especially against David, in an attempt to abort the coming of Messiah and the kingdom.

Paul quoted Psalm 69:23 as evidence that it had been fulfilled in his day through a remnant that God had preserved. (See Romans 11:10.) In this way, the imprecations in Psalms were judgments coming against those who fought against the kingdom. They were against the wicked who had opposed the kingdom from the time of David to the coming of Christ.

CHAPTER 2

THE INVISIBLE KING

THE KING IS eternal, immortal, and invisible. He is worthy of honor and glory forever and ever. He is the King of the ages and is to receive glory to the ages of the ages. *Invisible* means "incapable of being seen; inaccessible to view; hidden; imperceptible; inconspicuous."[1] In other words, the King cannot be seen with the natural eye. The King can only be seen with a spiritual eye to those to whom He chooses to reveal Himself.

> Now unto the King eternal, immortal, invisible, the only wise God, be honour and glory for ever and ever. Amen.
>
> —1 TIMOTHY 1:17, KJV

> ...and to the King of the ages, the incorruptible, invis-
> ible, only wise God, [is] honour and glory—to the ages
> of the ages! Amen.
>
> —1 TIMOTHY 1:17, YOUNG'S

Isaiah saw this king in a vision. Prophets were seers and had the ability to see into the spirit realm and experience what could not be seen with the natural eyes.

> In the year that King Uzziah died, I saw the Lord sit-
> ting on a throne, high and lifted up, and the train of His
> robe filled the temple. Above it stood seraphim; each
> one had six wings: with two he covered his face, with
> two he covered his feet, and with two he flew. And one
> cried to another and said: "Holy, holy, holy is the LORD
> of hosts; the whole earth is full of His glory!" And the
> posts of the door were shaken by the voice of him who
> cried out, and the house was filled with smoke. So I
> said: "Woe is me, for I am undone! Because I am a man
> of unclean lips, and I dwell in the midst of a people of
> unclean lips; for my eyes have seen the King, the LORD
> of hosts." Then one of the seraphim flew to me, having
> in his hand a live coal which he had taken with the
> tongs from the altar.
>
> —ISAIAH 6:1–6

Isaiah saw the King in His glory. The King was surrounded by seraphim that cried, "Holy, holy, holy." One of the major attributes of the invisible King is His *holiness*. His holiness sets Him apart from every other being.

John also saw the throne and the invisible King. John was in the Spirit when he saw the King. John saw the *holiness* of the King before he saw His *judgments*. The holiness of God is revealed before judgment comes to the land. The same is true in Revelation; John saw the holiness of the King before His judgments. God's judgments proceed from His holiness.

> After these things I looked, and behold, a door standing open in heaven. And the first voice which I heard was like a trumpet speaking with me, saying, "Come up here, and I will show you things which must take place after this." Immediately I was in the Spirit; and behold, a throne set in heaven, and One sat on the throne. And He who sat there was like a jasper and a sardius stone in appearance; and there was a rainbow around the throne, in appearance like an emerald. Around the throne were twenty-four thrones, and on the thrones I saw twenty-four elders sitting, clothed in white robes; and they had crowns of gold on their heads. And from the throne proceeded lightnings, thunderings, and voices. Seven lamps of fire were burning before the throne, which are the seven Spirits of God. Before the throne there was a sea of glass, like crystal. And in the midst of the throne, and around the throne, were four living creatures full of eyes in front and in back. The first living creature was like a lion, the second living creature like a calf, the third living creature had a face like a man, and the fourth living creature was like a flying eagle. The four living creatures, each having six wings, were full of eyes around and within. And they do not rest day or night, saying: "Holy, holy, holy, Lord God Almighty, Who was and is and is to come!"
>
> Whenever the living creatures give glory and honor and thanks to Him who sits on the throne, who lives forever and ever, the twenty-four elders fall down before Him who sits on the throne and worship Him who lives forever and ever, and cast their crowns before the throne, saying: "You are worthy, O Lord, To receive

> glory and honor and power; For You created all things,
> And by Your will they exist and were created."
>
> —REVELATION 4:1–11

The glory surrounding the throne is like a jasper, emerald, and sardius stone. John saw the beauty and glory of this invisible throne. Although it is invisible to the natural eye, it is nonetheless real. This glory emanates from the One sitting on the throne. Another characteristic of the invisible King is His *glory*. The King is holy and glorious. *Glory* means "great beauty or splendor."[2] *Splendor* means "great brightness or luster; brilliancy; magnificence; something splendid."[3] It indicates something grand or magnificent, of great fame and full of glory.

The throne is surrounded by worship. Angels and heavenly beasts worship at this throne, recognizing the holiness of the King. The throne is everlasting, and the One sitting on the throne lives forever and ever.

The invisible King is holy, wise, powerful, merciful, and majestic. His throne and kingdom are above all else. God permitted men to see His throne in the Spirit. The throne is real and governs the affairs of men. A revelation of the King and His throne will cause you to live a life pleasing and submitted to Him.

CHRIST IN MAJESTY

> The LORD reigns, He is clothed with majesty;
> The LORD is clothed,
> He has girded Himself with strength.
> Surely the world is established, so that it cannot be
> moved.
>
> —PSALM 93:1

The King is clothed in majesty. *Majesty* means "sovereign power, authority, or dignity; used in addressing or referring to royal sovereigns...royal bearing or aspect; grandeur; greatness or splendor of quality or character."⁴ Christ the Lord is clothed in majesty, which indicates a representation of Christ as ruler of the universe.

Those who saw the King in visionary form saw His majesty, glory, splendor, and holiness. They would fall on their faces or faint when encountering the glory and majesty of the King. In one of Ezekiel's visions of God he saw the throne:

> And above the firmament over their heads was the likeness of a throne, in appearance like a sapphire stone; on the likeness of the throne was a likeness with the appearance of a man high above it. Also from the appearance of His waist and upward I saw, as it were, the color of amber with the appearance of fire all around within it; and from the appearance of His waist and downward I saw, as it were, the appearance of fire with brightness all around. Like the appearance of a rainbow in a cloud on a rainy day, so was the appearance of the brightness all around it. This was the appearance of the likeness of the glory of the LORD. So when I saw it, I fell on my face, and I heard a voice of One speaking.
>
> —EZEKIEL 1:26–28, 2:1

Ezekiel also saw the colors of amber and sapphire and the appearance of fire and brightness. He saw a rainbow, a symbol of mercy. When he recognized that he was seeing the glory of the Lord, he fell upon his face. This has been the response of everyone who had a vision of the throne—they were overwhelmed.

In Daniel 7, we read of the vision of the invisible King and His throne that Daniel had. He watched the "Ancient of Days" take His place upon His throne and described what the Lord and His throne looked like in his vision.

> I watched till thrones were put in place,
> And the Ancient of Days was seated;
> His garment was white as snow,
> And the hair of His head was like pure wool.
> His throne was a fiery flame,
> Its wheels a burning fire;
> A fiery stream issued
> And came forth from before Him.
> A thousand thousands ministered to Him;
> Ten thousand times ten thousand stood before Him.
>
> —DANIEL 7:9–10

Daniel saw a throne like a fiery flame. This represents judgment that comes from the throne. God's throne is a throne of judgment. It is also a throne of mercy, symbolized by the rainbow that John saw around the throne.

Daniel also saw multitudes of holy angels, the attendants of the King and His throne. As his vision opened, Daniel saw the Son of Man coming to possess the throne (the kingdom).

> I was watching in the night visions,
> And behold, One like the Son of Man,
> Coming with the clouds of heaven!
> He came to the Ancient of Days,
> And they brought Him near before Him.
> Then to Him was given dominion and glory and a
>   kingdom,
> That all peoples, nations, and languages should serve
>   Him.
> His dominion is an everlasting dominion,
> Which shall not pass away,
> And His kingdom the one
> Which shall not be destroyed.
>
> —DANIEL 7:13–14

Each of these prophets who had visions of the throne were able to see into the Spirit realm and have a glimpse of an invisible King and His throne. There are millions of people who live and die without ever experiencing this kingdom, because it is not evident to the natural man or the five senses. But those who believe can access this kingdom by faith, enjoy the rule of this invisible King.

> I am the LORD, your Holy One, the Creator of Israel, your King.
>
> —ISAIAH 43:15

Although Israel's king was invisible, they saw manifestations of His power. Their King was their Savior, Protector, and Deliverer. They entered into a covenant with the King at Sinai and pledged their loyalty to Him. He, in turn, pledged His loyalty to them and promised to be their Provider, Protector, and Healer. Israel was the creation of the King.

THE KING'S LAW

The Law given to Israel at Sinai was the King's law. This law was to be supreme. It was to be followed without question. Breaking this law would bring the curse of the King; keeping this law would bring the blessing of the King. The Law represented the authority of the King. Disobedience and rebellion to the Commandments were disobedience and rebellion to the King. To disobey meant dishonor to the king and His law. Kings require honor. To dishonor a king is a grievous offense. A king's honor is paramount.

The Law was a covenant between the King and His subjects. Israel agreed to this covenant, and it was ratified at Sinai. There were two covenant seals given, which included circumcision and the Sabbath. The curses and blessings of the covenant are recorded in Deuteronomy.

When Israel violated the covenant, the King would warn them

of these covenant violations by sending His covenant messengers, the prophets. The prophets would call Israel back to covenant by warning them of impending covenant wrath and the need for repentance. To dishonor the King and His covenant resulted in judgment from the King through the attack of invading armies. The King used heathen nations to chastise Israel, for He is the Lord of hosts. In Isaiah 44:6 we read, "Thus says the LORD, the King of Israel, and his Redeemer, the LORD of hosts: 'I am the First and I am the Last; besides Me there is no God.'"

In this way, Israel therefore saw the invisible King's power and authority in judgment. These judgments proved the reality of the invisible King's rule over Israel and the nations.

> And ye shall be unto me a kingdom of priests, and an holy nation. These are the words which thou shalt speak unto the children of Israel.
>
> —EXODUS 19:6, KJV

They were called to be a kingdom of priests. They were called to be the ministers and servants of the king.

> "And you shall be to Me a kingdom of priests and a holy nation." These are the words which you shall speak to the children of Israel.
>
> —EXODUS 19:6

ISRAEL REJECTS THE KING

Israel rejected the invisible King. Israel was disobedient and unfaithful to the covenant its fathers made with the King. They were guilty of covenant violation and betrayal, and they served and worshiped other gods. They were not steadfast in the covenant. This historical rebellion—and its consequences—is well documented. The ultimate rejection came when Israel asked for a visible king. They desired to be like the nations who had visible kings. This was a turning point in their history. They did not listen to the warnings of what would happen to them with earthly kings. They would be oppressed. They would be taxed. They would be led away from serving the invisible King by ungodly kings.

Because of their rebellion and disobedience, the Lord told Samuel to warn them of the consequences they would face. In 1 Samuel 8:9, the Lord tells Samuel, "You shall solemnly forewarn them, and show them the behavior of the king who will reign over them." He was saying to them, "You asked Me for a king—well, this will be the result of your disobedience."

Their sons would be taken from them and appointed to serve in the army of the king, driving his chariots and running before him into battle. The king would appoint military leaders to rule over them. Some of their sons would be required to plow the ground and reap the harvest, and others would be assigned to make weapons for war and equipment for his chariots. (See 1 Samuel 8:11–12.)

Their daughters would be required to serve the king as perfumers, cooks, and bakers.

The king would take their best fields, vineyards, and olive groves and give them to his servants. He would require that they give a tenth of their grain and wine to his officers and servants.

The king would take the people's servants for his own, and their donkeys would do work for the king. He would take a tenth of their sheep as his own.

The consequences would be severe. Samuel told the people, "And you will cry out in that day because of your king whom you have chosen for yourselves, and the LORD will not hear you in that day" (1 Sam. 8:18). Nevertheless, the people refused to obey the voice of Samuel and continued to insist that they be given a king. Eventually the people would cry out to God because of the harsh rule of their earthly king, but He would not hear.

In His anger, the invisible King gave them an earthly king, even though He was not pleased with their request. However, when King Saul rejected God, in His wrath God removed him from the people. His rebellion was a manifestation of the rebellion of Israel. Although God granted Israel an earthly king, He was greatly displeased at their rebellion. In Hosea, God speaks of Israel as destroyed without Him as her King:

> O Israel, you are destroyed, but your help is from Me. I will be your King; where is any other, that he may save you in all your cities? And your judges to whom you said, "Give me a king and princes"? I gave you a king in My anger, and took him away in My wrath.
>
> —HOSEA 13:9–11

THE PROMISE OF A FUTURE KING

However, God did give them the promise of a future King who would rule and reign in righteousness. Through David, God promised a coming King. This King would be the invisible King manifested in the flesh. David and Solomon would be types of this coming King and His kingdom.

The prophets spoke of the coming King and His kingdom. One of the greatest prophecies is recorded by Isaiah:

> For unto us a Child is born, unto us a Son is given; and the government will be upon His shoulder. And His name will be called Wonderful, Counselor, Mighty God, Everlasting Father, Prince of Peace. Of the increase of His government and peace there will be no end, upon the throne of David and over His kingdom, to order it and establish it with judgment and justice

from that time forward, even forever. The zeal of the
LORD of hosts will perform this.

—ISAIAH 9:6–7

There are several things to note about this prophecy. The Son
that would be born would be the mighty God and the everlasting
Father. The kingdom to be established would continue to increase
and have no end. It would be established with justice and judgment. This is therefore a reference to a divine King whose kingdom
is not limited by an earthly life. The divine King would be an everlasting King not subject to mortality, which always ends earthly
kingdoms.

Therefore the kingdom is not an earthly one. It is not subject to defeat, overthrow, or end like earthly kingdoms. It is not an
earthly dynasty. Jesus made this plain when He told Pilate, "My
kingdom (kingship, royal power) belongs not to this world. If My
kingdom were of this world, My followers would have been fighting
to keep Me from being handed over to the Jews. But as it is, My
kingdom is not from here (this world); [it has no such origin or
source]" (John 18:36, AMP).

Jesus meant that His kingdom's origin was not from Earth.
It was the kingdom of heaven. The kingdom's source of power and
authority is from heaven, not Earth. The rules and standards of this
kingdom are high, because its source is high. Heaven is the highest
place, and its rules are higher than all. Jesus's source of power came
from above, and He therefore did not have to fight to establish His
kingdom.

A kingdom is simply the sphere where a king rules. Earthly kingdoms rule over earthly spheres or territories. These are areas where
the king's law is supreme. The people of those realms submit to the
king's law and honor the king. The king's authority in these realms is
absolute. Rebellion to the king's law and rule brings judgment. Those

who submit to the king's rule have the blessing of the king, and those who rebel face his wrath.

> The LORD has established His throne in heaven, and His kingdom rules over all.
>
> —PSALM 103:19

> The LORD is in His holy temple, the LORD's throne is in heaven; His eyes behold, His eyelids test the sons of men.
>
> —PSALM 11:4

These are significant verses. They give us the location of the throne. The throne is in heaven. It is a heavenly throne, not an earthly throne. It has absolute authority over all thrones and kingdoms. It is not subject to decay or ruin like earthly thrones and kingdoms.

David's earthly throne was only a type of the heavenly throne. David's earthly throne went into decay and ruin because of the sins of his sons. God promised to restore this throne and close up its breaches. The restoration of the throne is called the *rebuilding of the tabernacle of David*. This prophecy began to be fulfilled with the establishment of the church and is recorded in Acts 15. This is kingdom terminology and shows us that the kingdom that Jesus promised was at hand.

> Therefore, being a prophet, and knowing that God had sworn with an oath to him that of the fruit of his body, according to the flesh, He would raise up the Christ to sit on his throne, he, foreseeing this, spoke concerning the resurrection of the Christ, that His soul was not left in Hades, nor did His flesh see corruption. This Jesus God has raised up, of which we are all witnesses. Therefore being exalted to the right hand of God, and having received from the Father the promise of the Holy Spirit, He poured out this which you now see and

hear. For David did not ascend into the heavens, but
he says himself: "The LORD said to my Lord, 'Sit at My
right hand, Till I make Your enemies Your footstool.'"
Therefore let all the house of Israel know assuredly that
God has made this Jesus, whom you crucified, both
Lord and Christ.

—ACTS 2:30–36

How could the church be a fulfillment of the restoration of the
tabernacle of David? What is the connection of the church to the
throne of David? The answer is that Jesus ascended to sit on the heavenly throne and poured out the Holy Spirit at Pentecost. The church
was being formed as a result of His outpouring. The outpouring was
a sign that Jesus had occupied the heavenly throne and was ruling
and reigning over a new-creation people.

The throne of David could only be accessed through the
Resurrection. This is because the throne is a heavenly throne. Jesus
could not sit on this throne while He lived on Earth. His death and
resurrection were needed to ascend to the throne.

For if He were on earth, He would not be a priest, since
there are priests who offer the gifts according to the law.

—HEBREWS 8:4

Christ could not be an earthly priest because He was not
descended from Levi. He is a heavenly priest after the order of
Melchizedek. He ever lives as a priest to make intercession. He is the
King-Priest prophesied by Zechariah:

Yes, He shall build the temple of the LORD. He shall
bear the glory, and shall sit and rule on His throne; so
He shall be a priest on His throne, and the counsel of
peace shall be between them both.

—ZECHARIAH 6:13

He sits on a heavenly throne with a heavenly, kingly, priestly order after Melchizedek.

Ancient kings were often priests. They were considered intermediaries between the people and their gods. Christ is our King and Intercessor. There is no end to His rule or intercession.

Zechariah prophesied that Christ would build the temple of the Lord. The church is the temple of the Lord that He has built. We are the habitation of God through the Spirit.

The outpouring of the Spirit on the Day of Pentecost was a sign that Christ was sitting on the throne of David. This was the beginning of the restoration of the tabernacle of David, spoken of by the prophet Amos. David's ruined kingdom was being rebuilt, and it would be a kingdom that could never be ruined. God poured out His Spirit upon those who were under His rule. This began at Pentecost among the Jews who came under His rule and eventually was poured out upon the Gentiles who submitted to His rule.

Those who are in the kingdom and live under the king's rule can only do it by the Spirit. The Holy Spirit is the person who enables us to live kingdom lifestyles. By receiving the Spirit, we can walk in and live in the Spirit. Kingdom living is submitting to the leading of the Holy Spirit. Remember that Israel, after the flesh, could never submit to the rule of God. The promise of the Spirit is connected to the coming of the kingdom. In Romans 14:17 we read, "The kingdom of God is...in the Holy Spirit."

The power of the Holy Ghost was a sign that the kingdom was arriving. Jesus demonstrated this by casting out demons through the power of the Holy Ghost (Matt. 12:28). Many have not seen the connection between the Holy Spirit and the kingdom. The rule of God is through the Spirit. It is not a physical rule but a spiritual rule. The Holy Spirit is the ruling force of God. His influence is what causes people to submit. Men and women submit to God's will when they yield to the Holy Spirit. The invisible King rules through an invisible Spirit.

When Israel rebelled against the King, they vexed His Holy Spirit. He became their enemy instead of their protector King and fought against them.

> But they rebelled and grieved His Holy Spirit; so He turned Himself against them as an enemy, and He fought against them. Then he remembered the days of old, Moses and his people, saying: "Where is He who brought them up out of the sea with the shepherd of His flock? Where is He who put His Holy Spirit within them?
>
> —ISAIAH 63:10–11

Israel never submitted to the Holy Spirit God put within them. Israel was baptized in the cloud. This was a picture of being baptized in the Holy Spirit. God had set His Holy Spirit among them. They continually rebelled against His Spirit. They continually refused to listen to His voice, even though the presence of God was in their midst.

The new-creation people become the sphere of the King's rule and reign. They submit to His rule through the Holy Spirit, and they call Him Lord. This was always the purpose and plan of God from the foundation of the world. God desired a people who would submit to His rule. This people were to be formed in Christ. They would enter the kingdom by faith and be born from above. The kingdom is heavenly and spiritual and cannot be entered into by fleshly birth. It is a spiritual kingdom and can only be accessed by spiritual birth. The entire operation is by the Holy Spirit.

This is why the announcement of the kingdom by John, Christ, and the apostles coincides with the establishment of the church and the outpouring of the Holy Spirit. It is all kingdom related. The announcement of the kingdom of God was an announcement of salvation, redemption, outpouring, and the formation of a new-covenant community called the church. It is also the restoration of the tabernacle of David, where the Son of David would sit on a heavenly throne ruling and reigning over His people, both Jew and Gentile, in one body, His church.

The King who became visible would once again become invisible through His death and resurrection. He would sit on an invisible throne, and His kingdom would be invisible to the human eye.

CHAPTER 3

THE KING OF SAINTS

T HE LAMB IS the King of the saints. The *saints* are the holy
ones, those sanctified in Christ (1 Cor. 1:2). We are the saints
if we have called upon the name of Jesus and accepted His
grace and forgiveness. The saints possess the kingdom. The saints
are the ones who experience the righteousness, peace, and joy of the
kingdom (Rom. 14:17). This is the result of being in Christ. The saints
are the ones submitted to the rule of Christ the King through the
Spirit. They obey His voice and obey His Word. This is what true
kingdom living is all about. It is present now through Christ and the
Holy Spirit.

THE KING WHO SITS ON THE THRONE

It is important to link Old Testament prophecy to New Testament
fulfillment, especially when we are considering our invisible King.

Our King—the Lord our God—is a holy King, and many scriptures instruct us to worship Him *on high* or *at His holy hill* (Ps. 99:9). We receive greater revelation about this holy hill from Psalm 68.

> Is Mount Bashan the high mountain of summits, Mount Bashan [east of the Jordan] the mount of God? Why do you look with grudging and envy, you many-peaked mountains, at the mountain [of the city called Zion] which God has desired for His dwelling place? Yes, the Lord will dwell in it forever. The chariots of God are twenty thousand, even thousands upon thousands. The Lord is among them as He was in Sinai, [so also] in the Holy Place (the sanctuary in Jerusalem). You have ascended on high. You have led away captive a train of vanquished foes; You have received gifts of men, yes, of the rebellious also, that the Lord God might dwell there with them.
>
> —PSALM 68:15–18, AMP

Here we see a comparison between the mountains of Bashan and Zion, the mountain upon which God chose to establish His throne. The mountains of Bashan (including Mount Hermon) stood at the northern boundary between Judea and the heathen world. In many ways, Bashan is more beautiful and majestic than Zion. But Zion is compared to it because Zion is where God dwells.

Verse 17 describes God moving in His mighty chariots (as a victorious military leader) from Mount Sinai to Mount Zion. The conquering God takes His place on high in Zion and establishes His throne there.

Paul quotes from verse 18 of this psalm when describing spiritual gifts in Ephesians 4. By quoting this psalm, Paul is stating that Jesus is the King who now sits on the throne, ruling over the nations. But Paul amplified this psalm in a number of ways.

1. The psalm speaks about the ascension of a king to
   the throne over the enemies' armies (Ps. 68:18). Paul
   applies this meaning to Jesus but expands the meaning
   to include Jesus descending to the earth, His body
   being laid in a tomb, His resurrection, and His ascension back to the Father in heaven (Eph. 4:9–10).

2. The psalm speaks about the people, even the rebellious, bringing gifts to the king (v. 18). Paul applies
   this psalm to Christ, but rather than us giving gifts
   to Him, Christ is giving gifts to us. This is a natural
   interpretation of Psalm 68, because God has been
   pictured as being victorious over the nations and
   acquiring the spoils of victory. Paul is not denying this
   fact but is amplifying this truth. Christ is victorious
   over the nations and has acquired the spoils of victory.
   However, as King, Christ has distributed these spoils
   (or gifts) to the people (Eph. 4:7). Ephesians 4:11 names
   these gifts to include the apostles, prophets, evangelists, pastors, and teachers.

3. The final important implication, though unstated, is
   that in Psalm 68 we see God establishing His kingdom
   in Zion. Since Jesus is the Messiah, He is the fulfillment of this psalm. Jesus established the kingdom of
   God in Zion.

When did the establishment of the kingdom take place? Paul
indicates that His ascension made it possible for Him to "fill all
things" (Eph. 4:10). It ushered in His kingdom—He reigns from
His throne forevermore. This powerful link between Psalm 68 and
Ephesians 4 is emphasized by the closing words of Psalm 68: "O God,
You are more awesome than Your holy places" (v. 35).

The prophecies of Ezekiel confirm to us that the nations would know that the Lord is holy, and they will come and worship Him (Ezek. 39:7). Ezekiel is prophesying about judgment. No longer would God's holy name be polluted. Judgment came with the arrival of the kingdom, and the nations came to Zion to worship. We worship God because He is *holy*. His holiness was manifested by His judgment. The nations saw His righteousness and judgments.

There were other times in history when God's judgments caused the nations to recognize the God of Israel as the true God. (See Exodus 15:14–16.) This occurred after God's judgment on Pharaoh and Egypt. It also happened after the judgment upon Sennacherib and the Assyrian army. One judgment came through Moses and the other through Hezekiah, both types of Christ. God used these events to show His glory and power to the nations. Some commentators have ascribed the *reigning psalms* (Ps. 93–99) to the time of Israel and Hezekiah's deliverance from Sennacherib and the Assyrian army. An angel of the Lord slaughtered thousands, and the boasting of the Assyrians and their idols came to an end. These psalms reflect the superiority of the true God over the gods of the heathen. (See 2 Kings 18–19.)

The ends of the earth have seen the salvation of God. God made bare His holy arm in the sight of the nations, and the kingdom will bring salvation to the entire world (Isa. 52:10).

A PLACE OF WORSHIP AND PROPHECY

The hill of God is a place of worship and prophecy. It is a place of prophetic worship where men encounter the presence of God. This causes people to be changed by the Spirit of God.

> After that you shall come to the hill of God where the Philistine garrison is. And it will happen, when you have come there to the city, that you will meet a group of prophets coming down from the high place with a

The King of Saints

stringed instrument, a tambourine, a flute, and a harp before them; and they will be prophesying.

—1 SAMUEL 10:5

A ROD OF IRON

The nations are broken with a rod of iron.

You shall break them with a rod of iron; You shall dash them to pieces like a potter's vessel.

—PSALM 2:9

This is accomplished through the preaching of the Word of God, the sword of the Spirit. The nations are smitten with a sharp sword that comes out of the King's mouth (Rev. 19:15). The Word of God has judged more nations in history than any other force and will continue to do so. The preaching of the gospel is still the most powerful force in the world. It is the power of God unto salvation. Where the Word of the King is, there is power.

The rod of iron is a symbol of strength. "Rod" is the English translation of the Hebrew word *shebet*. This is also the shepherd's rod, which protects the sheep and smites the devourers. The rod is a symbol of government (Gen. 49:10, "ruler's staff"). The King will rule like a shepherd.

In Psalm 2 we find a powerful prophecy that says that the King is set on the throne in spite of the opposition from the heathen (Ps. 2:5–6). This opposition came from Herod, Pontius Pilate, the Gentiles, and even from the people of Israel.

The kings of the earth took their stand, and the rulers were gathered together against the LORD and against His Christ. For truly against Your holy Servant Jesus, whom You anointed, both Herod and Pontius Pilate, with the Gentiles and the people of Israel, were gathered together to do whatever Your hand and Your purpose determined before to be done.

—ACTS 4:26–28

God laughed at the efforts of men against the arrival of the kingdom. Man's feeble attempts to stop Jesus from being enthroned were stopped by the wisdom and purposes of God. The kingdom was not delayed or postponed. The opposition to the King was by the determined counsel of God. Jesus had to suffer and die to enter into His glory.

THE RULE OF GOD IS INWARD

Where there is no king, everyone makes his or her own rules and standards. Before God gave a king to the Israelites, "everyone did what was right in his own eyes" (Judg. 17:6). Those who are not submitted to the king have their own system of how to live. There are many philosophies of living that are accepted, and many of them are in rebellion to the rule of God.

The reign of God is in the hearts of men:

> It does not come with pomp and splendour, like the reign of temporal kings, merely to control the external "actions" and strike the senses of men with awe—but it reigns in the heart by the law of God; it sets up its dominion over the passions, and brings every thought into captivity to the obedience of Christ.[1]

God's law is placed in our hearts through the new covenant.

> But this is the covenant that I will make with the house of Israel after those days, says the LORD: I will put My law in their minds, and write it on their

hearts; and I will be their God, and they shall be My people.

—Jeremiah 31:33

God rules us through the establishment of His law in the heart. There are many places in Scripture that clearly show this.

But he is a Jew who is one inwardly; and circumcision is that of the heart, in the Spirit, not in the letter; whose praise is not from men but from God.

—Romans 2:29

Behold, You desire truth in the inward parts, and in the hidden part You will make me to know wisdom.

—Psalm 51:6

For I delight in the law of God according to the inward man.

—Romans 7:22

Then the Lord said to him, "Now you Pharisees make the outside of the cup and dish clean, but your inward part is full of greed and wickedness."

—Luke 11:39

The Pharisees were not submitted inwardly. They had the outward appearance of righteousness, but inwardly they were filled with wickedness. They were looking for an outward kingdom and missed the inward kingdom of Christ.

In the Old Testament, the tabernacle and temple were types of the kingdom. God dwelt in the holy of holies, positioned between the two cherubim on the ark of the covenant. From there He told Moses that He would speak with the Israelites "about everything which I will give you in commandment to the children of Israel"

(Exod. 25:22). The holy of holies was the *inward part* of the sanctuary. This represents the inward rule of God. God rules in the heart, the spirit—the hidden man of the heart.

The holy of holies was located behind the veil. The veil represents the flesh (Heb. 10:20). The hidden man of the heart is behind the veil of our flesh, and it cannot be seen with the natural eye. This is where God dwells and rules—in our heart, behind the veil of the flesh. Peter said "the hidden person of the heart, with the incorruptible beauty of a gentle and quiet spirit" was very precious in the sight of God (1 Pet. 3:4).

God's government is inward, not outward. Proverbs 25:28 tells us that "whoever has no rule over his own spirit is like a city broken down, without walls." He who does not govern his spirit is defenseless. This shows the necessity of inward government. Inward government affects outward action. A lack of inward government opens a person up to demonic influence.

God rules in the hearts of men. The kingdom of God is within. The Holy Spirit dwells within. The heart that is submitted to the Holy Spirit is under the rule of God.

The New Creation

The goal of the kingdom was the new creation. God would create a new people by the Spirit. Jesus is the foundation of this new people.

> Therefore, if anyone is in Christ, he is a new creation; old things have passed away; behold, all things have become new.
>
> —2 Corinthians 5:17

Jesus chose twelve apostles as the foundation of this new-covenant people. Twelve is the number of government. The twelve tribes were the foundation of the old-covenant nation, and the twelve apostles are the foundation of the new-covenant people.

The new creation would be a people created in Christ Jesus (Eph. 2:10). This new creation was prophesied by the prophets. It would consist of new people created through the new covenant. They would be a people created apart from fleshly descent and would be born from above. In other words, their birth would be *by the Spirit*, not from human effort.

> What is born of [from] the flesh is flesh [of the physical is physical]; and what is born of the Spirit is spirit. Marvel not [do not be surprised, astonished] at My telling you, You must all be born anew (from above). The wind blows (breathes) where it wills; and though you hear its sound, yet you neither know where it comes from nor where it is going. So it is with everyone who is born of the Spirit.
>
> —JOHN 3:6–8, AMP

Those birthed of the Spirit are born from above. This is the only way to be a citizen of heavenly Zion. (See Psalm 87:5–6.) It is entirely the work of the Holy Spirit and not the work of the flesh.

To be born in Zion is the greatest blessing. To be a citizen of Zion is the highest calling. Zion is a heavenly city, and those born in her are citizens of heaven. The Septuagint translation says, "Sion [Zion] is my mother."[2] The prophetic language of Isaiah 66:7–9 (AMP) speaks of the birth of the people of Zion:

> Before [Zion] travailed, she gave birth; before her pain came upon her, she was delivered of a male child. Who has heard of such a thing? Who has seen such things? Shall a land be born in one day? Or shall a nation be brought forth in a moment? For as soon as Zion was

in labor, she brought forth her children. Shall I bring
to the [moment of] birth and not cause to bring forth?
says the Lord. Shall I Who causes to bring forth shut
the womb? says your God.

Zion was birthed in a day. The church was birthed in a day—
on the Day of Pentecost. The church was brought forth in the midst
of persecution (pain, trouble, anguish). The Lord would not shut up
the womb. The church came forth, and the children of God were
birthed. Zion was birthed into the earth.

Barnes' Notes for Isaiah 66:8, "Shall a land be born in one day?
Or shall a nation be brought forth in a moment?" (AMP) states:

Such an event never has occurred. A nation is brought
into existence by degrees. Its institutions are matured
gradually, and usually by the long process of years.
But here is an event as remarkable as if a whole nation
should be born at once, and stand before the world,
mature in its laws, its civil institutions, and in all that
constitutes greatness. In looking for the fulfillment of
this, we naturally turn the attention to the rapid prog-
ress of the gospel in the times of the apostles, when
events occurred as sudden and as remarkable as if the
earth, after the desolation of winter or of a drought,
should be covered with rich luxuriance in a day, or as
if a whole nation should start into existence, mature in
all its institutions, in a moment.[3]

Matthew Henry further states:

The prophet...turns to those that trembled at his word,
to comfort and encourage them....God will appear to
the joy of the humble believer, and to the confusion
of hypocrites and persecutors....When the Spirit was

poured out, and the gospel went forth from Zion, multitudes were converted in a little time.[4]

In Isaiah 54:1–3 (KJV) we read:

> Sing, O barren, thou that didst not bear; break forth into singing, and cry aloud, thou that didst not travail with child: for more are the children of the desolate than the children of the married wife, saith the LORD. Enlarge the place of thy tent, and let them stretch forth the curtains of thine habitations: spare not, lengthen thy cords, and strengthen thy stakes; for thou shalt break forth on the right hand and on the left; and thy seed shall inherit the Gentiles, and make the desolate cities to be inhabited.

Sarah, the barren, is a type of the church. Israel would break out on the right hand and the left and inherit the Gentiles. The seed is Christ, who would inherit the nations. Galatians 4:26 (KJV) adds, "But Jerusalem which is above is free, which is the mother of us all." The freewoman is the heavenly Jerusalem.

The heavenly Jerusalem is our mother. We are born from above, from the freewoman. We are free from the law and have liberty. The barren women breaks forth with children in the nations. This is the kingdom—freedom, joy, rejoicing, and singing. The kingdom brings freedom from sin and death for the new creation.

The new-creation people would be those submitted to God's rule through the Holy Spirit. The old-creation people of God never submitted to the rule of God. Their consistent rebellion required the need for a new-creation people, born from above by the Holy Spirit.

When Jesus announced the nearness of the kingdom, He was announcing the nearness of the new creation. Jesus laid the foundation for this new people by choosing the twelve apostles as the foundation of this new nation.

God promised to create Jerusalem a rejoicing and her people a joy.

> But be glad and rejoice forever in what I create; for behold, I create Jerusalem as a rejoicing, and her people a joy.
>
> —ISAIAH 65:18

We are the new creation. We are the New Jerusalem created by God. We are the tabernacle (temple) of God. God has created us to be His dwelling place, His habitation.

The saints will rejoice forever in this new creation, from generation to generation and from age to age (Ps. 117:1–2). The New Jerusalem is an eternal city.

The nations would praise the Lord as a result of God's merciful kindness to Israel. In Romans 15:11, Paul quotes from the powerful words of Psalm 117 when he says: "Praise the LORD, all you Gentiles! Laud Him, all you peoples!"

God's mercy came upon Israel. God's salvation came to Israel. In Romans 15, Paul is speaking of the Gentile mission through His apostolic ministry. Notice the context:

> Now I say that Jesus Christ has become a servant to the circumcision for the truth of God, to confirm the promises made to the fathers, and that the Gentiles might glorify God for His mercy, as it is written: "For this reason I will confess to You among the Gentiles, and sing to Your name." And again he says: "Rejoice, O Gentiles, with His people!" And again: "Praise the LORD, all you Gentiles! Laud Him, all you peoples!" And again, Isaiah says: "There shall be a root of Jesse;

And He who shall rise to reign over the Gentiles, in
Him the Gentiles shall hope."

—ROMANS 15:8–12

Jesus came to confirm the promises to Israel (the circumcision). Jesus came to bring the promise of salvation and redemption
to Israel. When they saw this, the Gentiles would thank God for His
mercy and rejoice.

THE BANNER OF GOD'S PRESENCE

In Romans 8:12, Paul quoted from Isaiah 11:10 (KJV), which says,
"And in that day there shall be a root of Jesse, which shall stand for
an ensign of the people; to it shall the Gentiles seek: and his rest shall
be glorious." Paul saw the fulfillment of these promises in his day.

An *ensign* is a banner that is raised, causing people to assemble.
A banner gets the attention of people. The Gentiles would gather
under the banner of Christ. They would come to Zion, the New
Jerusalem. This depicts the *reign* of Christ over the Gentiles. The
nations would come under the reign of Christ and laud him. *Laud*
means "to praise, glorify, or extol."

Banners are a demonstration of God's presence lifted high in
our midst. One of the names of Christ is *Jehovah-Nissi, the Lord our
Banner*. After the Israelites' victory over the Amalekites, Moses built
an altar and named it "The-LORD-Is-My-Banner" (Exod. 17:15).

The *ensign* has been lifted; the *banner* has been raised. We have
seen it and have come to the *mountain* of the Lord to worship and
extol the King, Jehovah-Nissi, the Lord our Banner. We have been
drawn to the banner, to the kingdom, the mountain of God. We
extol the King (Ps. 145:1). This is the kingdom.

The King would be the suffering servant, the Messiah. The
kingdom is the reign of Messiah. He reigns in Zion, where His
banner is lifted. The nations come to Zion in praise of the King. The

redeemed of the Lord will sing for joy. The familiar words of Isaiah 51:11 talk of the joy expressed by the redeemed:

> So the ransomed of the LORD shall return,
> And come to Zion with singing,
> With everlasting joy on their heads.
> They shall obtain joy and gladness;
> Sorrow and sighing shall flee away.

We are the redeemed of the Lord who sing for joy. Zion (Jerusalem) is a place of joy and rejoicing. Sorrow and mourning flee. We have been redeemed by the blood of the Lamb.

> You were not redeemed with corruptible things, like silver or gold...but with the precious blood of Christ, as of a lamb without blemish and without spot.
> —1 PETER 1:18–19

We are the new creation. We have been created for God's glory. We are a people formed by the Lord. We have been created for *praise*. We are created in Christ for the *kingdom*.

CHAPTER 4

THE ROLE OF THE GOOD SHEPHERD

THE KINGDOM WOULD be a time when the Good Shepherd gathered His flock. Under the old covenant, the shepherds were negligent in their duties to feed and take care of the flock. They were *not ruling* the people properly. They were ruling the people with force and cruelty.

> Therefore thus says the LORD God of Israel against the shepherds who feed My people: "You have scattered My flock, driven them away, and not attended to them. Behold, I will attend to you for the evil of your doings," says the LORD.
>
> —JEREMIAH 23:2

The Day of the Lord would come upon these pastors because of their negligence. Jesus came to the lost sheep of the house of Israel.

He saw them scattered as sheep without a shepherd. Jesus came to gather, heal, and restore them. He identified Himself as the Good Shepherd.

THE GOOD SHEPHERD BRINGS REST AND SUSTENANCE

The Lord would bring His flock to the height of Zion. They would come to the goodness of the Lord, and He would provide them with wheat, wine, and oil. Their souls would be like a watered garden. Sorrow would flee away (Jer. 31:11–12). This would be the result of redemption. Jesus became the ransom. Because of His work of redemption, the sorrow of bondage departs. This is the blessing of salvation and liberty. This is the blessing of the kingdom.

In Ezekiel 34:15, the Good Shepherd affirms that He would feed His flock and would "make them lie down." *To lie down* means "to have a resting place." The kingdom is a place of rest. Jesus promised rest to those who came to Him (Matt. 11:28; Isa. 32:18). When we come to Christ we enter into rest. This is a place of spiritual rest. It is also a place of delight and provision.

This was the promise of God to His people—peaceable habitation and quiet resting places. This is the opposite of turmoil and worry. Christ is our resting place. Christ is our peaceable habitation. The rule of Christ, the Good Shepherd, gives us rest.

In the days of the prophets, many of the cities of Israel had become waste cities. This happened because Israel was taken captive by her enemies and forced to live in bondage in foreign cities. In Ezekiel 36:38 the prophet says when the kingdom of God was established, "so shall the ruined cities be filled with flocks of men." This is a picture of the restoration that our King will bring with His kingdom. In another prophecy, we see the King "will gather the lambs with His arm, and carry them in His bosom, and gently lead those who are with young" (Isa. 40:11).

When Jesus speaks to His disciples in Luke 12:32, He calls them His "little flock." They were the ones who would receive the kingdom. We are the Lord's flock. We are the sheep of His pasture. We are the ones who receive the kingdom. We are His church.

THE WORK OF THE CHURCH

The Good Shepherd was concerned that His flock would be well taken care of by those to whom He assigned the responsibility of overseer.

> Therefore take heed to yourselves and to all the flock, among which the Holy Spirit has made you overseers, to shepherd the church of God which He purchased with His own blood.
>
> —ACTS 20:28

The elders (bishops, overseers) are the ones responsible to feed the flock. The flock is the redeemed of the Lord. The local church is to be a pasture for the flock. A pasture is a meadow, a field of grass or other vegetation for the purpose of feeding grazing animals.[1] The Lord leads us to green pastures. The local church is a place where the sheep are fed the Word of God.

Therefore the church is the place in the kingdom where the sheep come to be fed and tended. This was the goal of the prophets. They saw a day when the sheep would be gathered and taken care of. The neglect and negligence of the old-covenant shepherds would come to an end. We now live under the rule of the Good Shepherd: "Know that the LORD, He is God; it is He who has made us, and not we our-selves; we are His people and the sheep of His pasture" (Ps. 100:3).

Jesus came to redeem the sheep who had gone astray (Isa. 53:6).

Our iniquity was placed on Him. Jesus came to redeem and gather the sheep into the sheepfold. The Good Shepherd gave His life for the sheep. He leads us beside the still waters. He restores our soul. He leads us in the path of righteousness.

Jesus came to seek and save that which was lost (Luke 19:10; Ezek. 34:11). Jesus sent the Twelve to seek after the sheep. Then Jesus sent the Seventy to seek after the sheep. Jesus still sends preachers to seek after the sheep. The kingdom is a time of gathering.

Jesus was moved with compassion when He saw that they had been scattered like sheep having no shepherd (Matt. 9:36). The sending of the Twelve came after Jesus saw the multitudes. The disciples were given power to heal the sick and cast out devils. In other words, He sent His disciples with the ability to do something about the condition of the sheep. This is in fulfillment of what Jeremiah and Ezekiel prophesied. It is a sign of the time of the kingdom.

Gentile Sheep

Jesus was very clear in His teachings that the Jews were not the only sheep. There were other sheep—outside the fold of Judaism—who needed to be brought into the fold also (John 10:16). He told His disciples that these other sheep would also hear His voice and would follow Him. He would create just one *sheepfold*, and there would be just one Shepherd.

He would rule over His flock. Feeding is a part of ruling. *To pastor* means "to feed." The word *pastor* comes from the Hebrew word *ra'ah*, meaning "to pasture, tend, graze, feed, to tend, pasture, to shepherd, *ruler*, teacher of people as flock, a herdsman."[2] King David was a shepherd, but Jesus, the greater David, is the Good Shepherd, the Good Ruler.

THE KINGDOM IS THE RULE OF THE GOOD SHEPHERD

The kingdom is therefore the rule of the Good Shepherd over His flock, the church. The sheep are gathered through evangelism and fed through teaching. As His restored sheep, we have returned to the Bishop and Shepherd of our souls. It is the ruling aspect of the role of the Good Shepherd that links the church and the kingdom together. Just as a shepherd feeds, guards, and cares for a flock, ruling over it, so too our Good Shepherd rules over His kingdom sheep.

In the time of the prophets, the shepherds were ruling the people with force and cruelty. They had not strengthened the diseased or healed the sick. They had not brought back those who had been driven away. They had not sought after the lost (Ezek. 34:4). This is why Jesus came as the Good Shepherd. He came to end the rule of the cruel shepherds and to bring in the rule of the Good Shepherd.

The pastures of the kingdom are places of shouting for joy and singing (Ps. 65:13). The kingdom's pastures are local churches where the flocks enjoy the blessings of the kingdom.

The people who seek after God are the people who seek the kingdom. In Isaiah 65:10, a prophecy says that they will inhabit Sharon. Sharon was a portion of land located south of Mount Carmel along the coast of the Mediterranean Sea. It extended from Caesarea to Joppa. In Scripture, this is almost always a proverbial name that denotes extraordinary beauty and fertility.

The kingdom of the Good Shepherd is filled with the glory of our invisible King. It will last from generation to generation. The Good Shepherd's flock will show forth the praises of the King throughout the world. As the sheep of His pasture, we praise Him for His salvation, redemption, healing, and deliverance.

CHAPTER 5

THE CHARACTERISTICS OF THE KINGDOM

THE KINGDOM IS filled with the glory of its king. As we look at Old Testament prophecy, we are able to identify some of the characteristics of this glorious kingdom. In this chapter we take a closer look at six important elements that characterize life in the kingdom—salvation, praise and worship, a highway to Zion, the river of God, a new covenant, and an increase of peace. Each of these is reflected in the lives of those who live in the kingdom and are beacons of light to lead others to kingdom living.

SALVATION

> How beautiful upon the mountains are the feet of him who brings good news, who proclaims peace, who

> brings glad tidings of good things, who proclaims
> salvation, who says to Zion, "Your God reigns!"
>
> —ISAIAH 52:7

The gospel is the good news of the reign of God. Those who hear, believe, and submit to the gospel are submitting themselves to the rule of God. Those who reject the gospel are rejecting the rule of God.

There is only one gospel. It is the gospel of the kingdom, the gospel of Christ, the everlasting gospel, and the gospel of peace. Jesus sent the Twelve and the Seventy to preach and demonstrate the gospel. The people in those cities who did not hear would come under judgment. Those who rejected the authority and rule of the King would experience His judgment.

> Then He began to rebuke the cities in which most of
> His mighty works had been done, because they did not
> repent: "Woe to you, Chorazin! Woe to you, Bethsaida!
> For if the mighty works which were done in you had
> been done in Tyre and Sidon, they would have repented
> long ago in sackcloth and ashes. But I say to you, it will
> be more tolerable for Tyre and Sidon in the day of judg-
> ment than for you."
>
> —MATTHEW 11:20–22

But for those who do repent and receive the gospel, the kingdom is a place of salvation and deliverance. Those who call on the name of the Lord receive deliverance, just as the prophets prophesied (Joel 2:32).

With the arrival of the kingdom came the arrival of salvation. Christ the King is also Christ the Savior. Kings save and deliver. Earthly kings could only bring temporal salvation, but the heavenly King brings eternal salvation. There is *deliverance* on Mount Zion. Those who come to Zion by faith are *saved*.

In Joel 2:32 (AMP) we see a reference to a remnant that escapes from captivity. Joel describes the remnant this way: "In Mount Zion and in Jerusalem there shall be those who escape, as the Lord has said, and among the remnant [of survivors] shall be those whom the Lord calls."

In the historical context, the remnant of Jews who came to Mount Zion was saved. Zion was the only place of safety and protection. They were the survivors of the judgment that came. *Salvation* is from the Greek word *sōtēria*, meaning "deliverance, preservation, safety, salvation, deliverance from the molestation of enemies, Messianic salvation."[1]

Salvation was the message of the prophets since the world began. Jesus came to save Israel from her enemies. This was the hope of the kingdom; this is what the people were longing for. This was the mercy promised to the fathers. This was the covenant God made with their fathers. God's covenant loyalty caused Him to act and send the Messiah. The kingdom brought eternal salvation.

> And having been perfected, He became the author of eternal salvation to all who obey Him.
>
> —Hebrews 5:9

Zion is also a place for saviors (deliverers). In Obadiah 21 we read, "Then saviors shall come to Mount Zion to judge the mountains of Esau, and the kingdom shall be the Lord's." The Book of Obadiah is written about the Edomites, who were ancient enemies of Israel. Edom represents the flesh. The flesh always opposes the Spirit, and the Edomites represent opposition to the kingdom. Their opposition was judged, and the kingdom was established.

Believers are deliverers. We are sent to bring salvation to the lost. We are sent to preach and minister deliverance to the captives. God used the apostles as deliverers, and they brought salvation through their preaching and teaching.

PRAISE AND WORSHIP

Zion is a place for worshipers. King David established Israel's worship in earthly Zion. He brought the ark of God to Jerusalem and placed it under a tent. He commanded the Levites to worship and praise continually. He established prophetic worship with the families of Heman, Asaph, and Jeduthun. (See 1 Chronicles 25.)

David established praise and worship in Zion. Davidic worship was a picture of what would one day happen worldwide. Davidic worship included:

- Singers and singing (1 Chron. 15:16–27; 25:1–7)

- Musicians and instruments (1 Chron. 23:5; 25:1–7)

- Ministry of Levites before the ark (1 Chron. 16:6, 37)

- Recording (1 Chron. 16:4; 28:12, 19)

- Thanking the Lord (1 Chron. 16:4, 8, 41)

- Praise (1 Chron. 16:4, 36)

- Psalms (1 Chron. 16:9; Ps. 98:6)

- Rejoicing and joy (1 Chron. 16:10, 16, 25, 31)

- Clapping hands (Ps. 47:1; 98:8; Isa. 55:12)

- Shouting (1 Chron. 15:28; Ps. 47:1, 5; Isa. 12:6)

- Dancing (1 Chron. 15:29; 2 Sam. 6:14; Ps. 149:3; 150:4)

- Lifting up hands (Ps. 134; 141:2; Lam. 3:41)

- Worship, bowing down (1 Chron. 16:29; Ps. 29:1–2; 95:6)

- Seeking the Lord (1 Chron. 16:10–11; 2 Chron. 7:14)

- Spiritual sacrifices (Ps. 27:6; Heb. 13:15–16; 1 Pet. 2:3–5)

- Saying "amen" (1 Chron. 16:36)

The establishment of worship by David was a type of global worship that would come through Christ. We are now living in the day of global worship. The arrival of the kingdom meant the arrival of global worship. Isaiah prophesied of the day when the Gentiles would become Levites. (See Isaiah 66:19–21.) The Levites were the priestly tribe. They were God's attendants. The Levites were appointed by David to minister before the ark in Zion.

As members of the kingdom, we are all the carriers of the ark of God. Just as the Levites were a gift to Israel, so too the fivefold ministry today is a gift to the church.

> Behold, I Myself have taken your brethren the Levites from among the children of Israel; they are a gift to you, given by the LORD, to do the work of the tabernacle of meeting.
>
> —NUMBERS 18:6

New-covenant saints are priests. We are carriers of the glory. We attend to the presence of God. We are God's attendants and servants. We minister before the Lord in Zion.

In the kingdom we are priests clothed with salvation. We shout for joy (Ps. 132:16). The priesthood would no longer be limited to descendants of Aaron but would be opened to all people. This is Zion. The priests minister in Zion, the city of God, the temple of the Lord, the place of God's habitation.

When He met and ministered to the woman at the well in Samaria, Jesus spoke of the day when worship would longer be centralized at the earthly mountain of geographical Jerusalem:

> Jesus said to her, "Woman, believe Me, the hour is coming when you will neither on this mountain, nor in Jerusalem, worship the Father."
>
> —JOHN 4:21

Worship is now taking place in the kingdom at the heavenly mountain of Zion, the church. God has moved from the physical mountain to the spiritual mountain.

The arrival of the kingdom meant that the nations would respond to God's government and would worship the King: "All the ends of the world shall remember and turn to the LORD, and all the families of the nations shall worship before You. For the kingdom is the LORD's, and He rules over the nations" (Ps. 22:27–28). True worshipers worship in Spirit and truth. The emphasis here is upon worship. Worship will go to the ends of the world, to the uttermost parts of the earth.

The prophets saw the nations worshiping with the arrival of the kingdom.

> Let the peoples praise You, O God;
> Let all the peoples praise You.
> Oh, let the nations be glad and sing for joy!
> For You shall judge the people righteously,
> And govern the nations on earth. Selah.
> Let the peoples praise You, O God;
> Let all the peoples praise You.
>
> —PSALM 67:3–5

This is *global gladness.* The worship of kingdom dwellers is to be "joyful noise" in the kingdom. We are to serve our invisible King with "gladness" and come into His presence with "singing" (Ps. 100:1–2).

Psalms 65 through 67 show a concern that all the nations would come to a true knowledge of God—not just that God's people in Israel would know the true God and love Him and worship Him and serve Him but that God and His people in Israel long for all the peoples of the world to come to a saving knowledge of Him. And so, these psalms are very much based around the promise of God to Abraham in Genesis 12:1–3. It is not only a promise that God will be a blessing to Abraham but also that Abraham would become a blessing to all the families of the earth.

Psalms 93 through 99 are a set of Messianic kingdom psalms, with many statements concerning the Lord's ruling and reigning. In them we learn to rejoice and be glad. We understand the blessing that the arrival of the kingdom is, and we shout with joy as we consider the salvation of our king.

Our shout is one of "Jehovah reigns!" (1 Chron. 16:31.) This is the cry of the kingdom. The heavens are glad, and the earth rejoices. The whole earth rejoices at Christ's salvation. We rejoice for the deliverance and healing that come with redemption. The fact that the God of Israel is worshiped by the nations is the ultimate triumph of Israel.

A Highway to Zion

Another characteristic of the kingdom is the fact the God has given us a clear road map for entering the kingdom—all nations will find their way into the kingdom via Christ, who is the highway to Zion, the *highway to holiness.*

> A highway shall be there, and a road, and it shall be called the Highway of Holiness. The unclean shall not pass over it, but it shall be for others. Whoever walks the road, although a fool, shall not go astray.
> —Isaiah 35:8

A highway is a main road for travel by the public between important destinations such as cities, large towns, and states. There is no more important highway than the one that leads to Zion.

God promised to make a way. The way He makes would be a new thing (Isa. 43:19). God would make a way in the wilderness. The *wilderness* represents sin. John the Baptist called Israel to the wilderness to repent (Matt. 3:3).

It is possible for anyone to find the highway to Zion. Isaiah said "whoever...although a fool" could find it. The blind would find the way to Zion. Those who sat in darkness would see the light. The crooked things would be made straight. This is the *geography of salvation*. God prepares a way in the wilderness of sin.

The highway to Zion leads out of darkness into the light. The light of Israel would come. He would be a light to illuminate the way for the Gentiles and would become the glory of Israel. The kingdom would come and bring the people out of darkness. This was the hope of Israel; this was the promise of the prophets.

The highway leads to Zion, which is a holy place for holy people. The saints are the holy people of the Lord. The Lord would sanctify His name through judgment and sanctify His people. This is both the judgment and the salvation that came at the end of the old covenant age.

The nations would come to Zion and live under the rule of the King as a result of judgment. God would magnify and sanctify Himself in the eyes of many nations: "Thus I will magnify Myself and sanctify Myself, and I will be known in the eyes of many nations. Then they shall know that I am the LORD" (Ezek. 38:23). The nations would know the Lord through His judgments upon the old-covenant system. God exercised His rule over Israel by judging them for apostasy.

This is the first-century context of the message "repent, for the kingdom of heaven is at hand." *Clarke's Commentary on the Bible* explains further by stating, "The Jews imagined that when the Messiah should come he would destroy the Gentiles, and reign gloriously over the Jews: the very reverse of this, our Lord intimates, should be the case. He was about to destroy the whole Jewish polity, and reign gloriously among the Gentiles. Hence he mentions the case of the general deluge, and the destruction of Sodom and Gomorrah. As if he had said: 'The coming of this kingdom shall be as fatal to you as the deluge was to the old world, and as the fire and brimstone from heaven were to Sodom and Gomorrah.' Our Lord states that this kingdom of heaven was within them, i.e. that they themselves should be the scene of these desolations, as, through their disobedience and rebellion, they possessed the seeds of these judgments."[2]

By getting on the highway to Zion, we can ride upon the high places and live on the mountain of God (Isa. 58:14). This is kingdom living. There is no highway on Earth that could compare to the highway to Zion. There are no detours or potholes. The road is brightly lit by the glorious presence of our invisible king.

The highway leads to the highest place. Zion is in the heights. God rules from the heights. The various synonyms for the word *heights* emphasize that there is no higher place than Zion. They include *tallness, stature, elevation, altitude, loftiness, pinnacle, summit, peak, top, apex, acme,* and *zenith.* There is no higher place than Zion. We have been brought to the summit through Christ.

> The Sovereign Lord is my strength; he makes my feet like
> the feet of a deer, he enables me to tread on the heights.
> —Habakkuk 3:19, niv

The River of God

Characteristic of the kingdom of our King is also the presence of a mighty river that flows from Zion and waters all the wilderness areas of our lives. The prophet Isaiah spoke of this river by saying, "I will make rivers flow on barren heights, and springs within the valleys. I will turn the desert into pools of water, and the parched ground into springs" (Isa. 41:18, niv).

Rivers flow from high places. Water comes down the mountains and waters the valleys. The river of God flows from Zion, the high place, the mountain of God. The streams that extend out of this river bring gladness to the city of God (Ps. 46:4).

Joel prophesied about the rivers of Judah, speaking of the river that flows in Zion. This is the river of God. Ezekiel saw this river coming from the temple. Wherever the river flows, it brings life. This river flows in Zion and brings joy and gladness. Ezekiel prophesied about God's promise to make rivers in the desert. Those in dry places would come into contact with this river, which causes death to flee and new life to be released.

> Along the bank of the river, on this side and that, will grow all kinds of trees used for food; their leaves will not wither, and their fruit will not fail. They will bear fruit every month, because their water flows from the sanctuary. Their fruit will be for food, and their leaves for medicine.
>
> —Ezekiel 47:12

The prophet Zechariah made a similar prediction:

> And in that day it shall be that living waters shall flow from Jerusalem, half of them toward the eastern sea and half of them toward the western sea; in both summer and winter it shall occur. And the LORD shall be King over all the earth.
>
> —Zechariah 14:8–9

This would be the day when the Lord would be *King* over all the earth. This is a picture of the kingdom. The kingdom age is a time when the river of God flows to the nations, bringing healing and life.

It is interesting to note that there are some places that will not be healed but will instead be turned to salt: "But its swamps and marshes will not be healed; they will be given over to salt"

(Ezek. 47:11). The river does not flow into the swamps and marshes. Historically, there are areas of the world that have not been touched by Ezekiel's river. This also is applicable on a personal level; there are some people who will be untouched by the river of God.

As the river flows, there will be obstacles and hindrances that prevent the river from flowing on. When a river stops flowing, it forms into lakes, swamps, and marshes. For example, the Dead Sea is no good to anyone because the water is too salty for any use. It cannot be used for drinking. It cannot be used for providing nutrients to the growth of plants and food. It is basically useless. In our lives, we must beware of swamps and marshes that hinder our personal relationship with God. These swamps and marshes prevent the power of the Holy Spirit flowing through us to others. When these swamps and marshes are built up over time, nothing living can grow in them. When we walk away from God and refuse the working of the Holy Spirit in our lives, we are like the swamps and marshes. No life will flow from us, and everything we touch does not bring life and draw others to God.

The river of God also flows out of our innermost being. Jesus said, "He who believes in Me, as the Scripture has said, out of his heart will flow rivers of living water" (John 7:38). This river is a supernatural river. God is in the midst of this river. It brings healing, and it produces fruit. As the Spirit flows out of our lives, we produce the fruit of the kingdom also.

The first mention of a river is connected to Eden (Gen. 2:10). Adam was expelled from Eden. Isaiah uses Eden as a picture of the kingdom. Isaiah spoke of Zion becoming an Eden. The language of the prophets is poetic and filled with powerful symbolic language.

> For the LORD will comfort Zion, He will comfort all
> her waste places; He will make her wilderness like
> Eden, and her desert like the garden of the LORD; joy

and gladness will be found in it, thanksgiving and the
voice of melody.

—ISAIAH 51:3

Our waste places become like Eden when we come into contact with the river of God. We become the garden of the Lord. We
have gladness, thanksgiving, and the voice of melody. Eden needs
a river. The river brings restoration and healing. This is a picture
of desolate lives being restored through the power of the kingdom.
We go from barrenness to fruitfulness when we are touched by the
river of God.

> You visit the earth and water it,
> You greatly enrich it;
> The river of God is full of water;
> You provide their grain,
> For so You have prepared it.
> You water its ridges abundantly,
> You settle its furrows;
> You make it soft with showers,
> You bless its growth.
>
> You crown the year with Your goodness,
> And Your paths drip with abundance.
> They drop on the pastures of the wilderness,
> And the little hills rejoice on every side.
> The pastures are clothed with flocks;
> The valleys also are covered with grain;
> They shout for joy, they also sing.

—PSALM 65:9–13

The river of God that flows from Zion releases blessing wherever it goes. This is the visitation of God.

A NEW COVENANT

The kingdom would mean the arrival of the new covenant. The promise of the new covenant is one of the most important in all of Scripture. Jeremiah's prophecy about a better covenant is mentioned by Paul in his letter to the Hebrews:

> But now He has obtained a more excellent ministry, inasmuch as He is also Mediator of a better covenant, which was established on better promises. For if that first covenant had been faultless, then no place would have been sought for a second. Because finding fault with them, He says: "Behold, the days are coming, says the LORD, when I will make a new covenant with the house of Israel and with the house of Judah—not according to the covenant that I made with their fathers in the day when I took them by the hand to lead them out of the land of Egypt; because they did not continue in My covenant, and I disregarded them, says the LORD. For this is the covenant that I will make with the house of Israel after those days, says the LORD: I will put My laws in their mind and write them on their hearts; and I will be their God, and they shall be My people. None of them shall teach his neighbor, and none his brother, saying, 'Know the LORD,' for all shall know Me, from the least of them to the greatest of them. For I will be merciful to their unrighteousness, and their sins and their lawless deeds I will remember no more." In that He says, "A new covenant," He has made the first obsolete. Now what is becoming obsolete and growing old is ready to vanish away.
>
> —HEBREWS 8:6–13

The old covenant was in the process of vanishing away when the letter to the Hebrews was written. The writer is revealing the superiority of the new covenant to the old. The priesthood is better (*Melchizedek*, "eternal"), and the covenant is better. This was necessary because some Hebrew believers were forsaking the church and returning to the old covenant system, which was about to be done away with completely.

This new covenant was necessary because of the continual violation of the old covenant by Israel. God would do a new thing and put His law in their inward parts. The new covenant is *inward*. The new covenant would also mean the removal of sin. In other words, eternal salvation would come through the new covenant.

God's rule (the kingdom) would be established through the new covenant.

INCREASE OF PEACE

The last characteristic of the kingdom—and one of the most desired—is the increase of peace within the kingdom of our King.

> I will make a covenant of peace with them, and cause wild beasts to cease from the land; and they will dwell safely in the wilderness and sleep in the woods.
> —EZEKIEL 34:25

This refers literally to a covenant of Shalom. *Shalom* means "completeness, wholeness, health, peace, welfare, safety soundness, tranquility, prosperity, perfectness, fullness, rest, harmony, the absence of agitation or discord." In the verse above, "wild beasts" represent evil spirits. In other words, the new covenant is a covenant of *peace*. Jesus is the Prince of Peace (Isa. 9:6).

The arrival of the kingdom is the arrival of the new covenant and the arrival of *peace*. Israel never enjoyed true, lasting peace under the old covenant. What they needed was forgiveness and the true peace of God.

> You will keep him in perfect peace, whose mind is stayed on You.
>
> —Isaiah 26:3

David Guzik writes:

> Perfect peace! God promises that we can have perfect peace, and even be kept in a place of perfect peace. In Hebrew the term *perfect peace* is actually *shalom shalom*....In Hebrew, repetition communicates intensity. It isn't just *shalom*; it is *shalom shalom*, "perfect peace."[3]

The coming of the kingdom would bring perfect peace, or *shalom shalom*. We can have double *shalom* in the kingdom.

CHAPTER 6

PROPHETIC VISIONS OF THE KINGDOM

MANY OF THE prophetic visions in the Bible about the coming of the kingdom of God can be found in the writings of Jeremiah and Isaiah. Through their writings we can get a glimpse not only of the glorious kingdom of God that would be established by our invisible King but also of the moral decline of the nation of Israel into total rebellion and disobedience and turning from God.

As we look at the prophetic visions of these two prophets, it will be helpful to also consider the critical historical periods during which each man lived.

THE KINGDOM ACCORDING TO ISAIAH

The ministry of Isaiah took place before the ministry of Jeremiah. Isaiah was apparently a highly esteemed citizen of Jerusalem who enjoyed access to the royal court. He was a trusted advisor of King Hezekiah. His ministry extended from the year of King Uzziah's death in 740 B.C. to the reign of the idolatrous King Manasseh, in whose persecution he was probably martyred. It was during this critical period of the latter half of the eighth century that Israel, the Northern Kingdom, suffered a swift and catastrophic decline. By the time that Manasseh came to the throne, an atmosphere of corruption and depravity covered the land. During this time, Isaiah received a series of prophetic revelations looking forward to the coming of the kingdom of God.[1]

The emphasis of Isaiah's prophetic visions is that foreigners would be a part of Israel's restoration. This most likely would have been a hard message for the people of Israel to hear at that time. Although they were sinking deeper and deeper into sin, they were still the chosen people of God—the only people of God—and it was the Gentile nations and *foreigners* who were persecuting and attacking them.

A call to Gentiles

But Isaiah is very clear in his prophecies that God Himself would call the Gentile nations to Himself. In Isaiah 5:26 he says, "He will lift up a banner to the nations from afar, and will whistle to them from the end of the earth." It was Jesus Christ who became this Banner. As I said before, one of the names of Christ is *Jehovah-Nissi, the Lord our Banner.* Isaiah prophesied of this banner when he said:

> And in that day there shall be a Root of Jesse, who shall stand as a banner to the people; for the Gentiles shall seek Him.
>
> —ISAIAH 11:10

The Lord our Banner would open the way for all peoples to become a part of His kingdom. While Jesus was on Earth He told

His followers, "But I, when I am lifted up from the earth, will draw all men to myself" (John 12:32, NIV). Isaiah prophesies of this with words from the King, who speaks of His call to the Gentiles: "I revealed myself to those who did not ask for me; I was found by those who did not seek me. To a nation that did not call on my name, I said, 'Here am I, here am I'" (Isa. 65:1).

Another prophecy in the words of our King Himself says:

> Behold, I will lift My hand in an oath to the nations, and set up My standard for the peoples; they shall bring your sons in their arms, and your daughters shall be carried on their shoulders; kings shall be your foster fathers, and their queens your nursing mothers; they shall bow down to you with their faces to the earth, and lick up the dust of your feet. Then you will know that I am the LORD, for they shall not be ashamed who wait for Me.
>
> —ISAIAH 49:22–23

The call into the kingdom would be clearly heard by all nations. Isaiah speaks in strong language when he says, "Come near, you nations, and listen; pay attention, you peoples! Let the earth hear, and all that is in it, the world, and all that comes out of it!" (Isa. 34:1, NIV). He issued a clear message to anyone reluctant to let the people come to God by saying: "I will say to the north, 'Give them up!' and to the south, 'Do not hold them back'" (Isa. 43:6, NIV).

Through the prophecies of Isaiah we see a clear picture of the inclusion of the Gentiles in the restoration of Israel and the establishment of the kingdom of God. It was God's desire that all peoples know the way into His kingdom. The words of Isaiah 62:10–12 (NIV) stress the importance of understanding that Jesus our King will draw all men unto Himself:

> Pass through, pass through the gates! Prepare the way
> for the people. Build up, build up the highway! Remove
> the stones. Raise a banner for the nations. The LORD
> has made proclamation to the ends of the earth: "Say to
> Daughter Zion, 'See, your Savior comes! See, his reward
> is with him, and his recompense accompanies him.'"
> They will be called the Holy People, the Redeemed of
> the LORD; and you will be called Sought After, the City
> No Longer Deserted.

The Gentiles would come and rebuild their walls (Isa. 60:10). The wealth of the seas and the wealth of the Gentiles would come to Israel. The desolations of many generations would be rebuilt by the coming in of the Gentiles. The nations would be blessed through Israel's restoration.

The people of Israel would take an active part in the expansion of the kingdom to include all peoples. Isaiah's prophetic words to the nation of Israel include a clear message that the people of Israel would become a light to lead the way for the Gentiles to find their way into the kingdom: "I will also make you a light for the Gentiles, that you may bring my salvation to the ends of the earth" (Isa. 49:6).

The prophecies of Isaiah tell the people of Israel clearly that God is not turning His back on them, even though they had turned their backs on Him. Isaiah says, "Wash and make yourselves clean. Take your evil deeds out of my sight! Stop doing wrong, learn to do right!...Zion will be redeemed with justice, her penitent ones with righteousness" (Isa. 1:16–17, 27, NIV). He promises those who turn back to God:

> I, the LORD, have called You in righteousness, and will
> hold Your hand; I will keep You and give You as a cov-
> enant to the people, as a light to the Gentiles.
>
> —ISAIAH 42:6

A vision of life in the kingdom

Some of the prophecies of Isaiah offered a picture of what life in the kingdom would be like. In Isaiah 11:1–9 he described the peaceful kingdom, teaching that even the animal kingdom would be at peace with one another. Then he says, "The earth shall be full of the knowledge of the LORD" (v. 9). In another scripture we eavesdrop on the conversation between the two seraphim who called him to the office of prophet:

> And one cried to another and said: "Holy, holy, holy is
> the LORD of hosts; the whole earth is full of His glory!"
> —ISAIAH 6:3

Everyone in the kingdom will continually praise the King. Isaiah writes, "From the ends of the earth we have heard songs: 'Glory to the righteous!'" (Isa. 24:16). In a later chapter, he says that the Lord will let the whole world know that there is none besides Him "from the rising of the sun to its setting" (Isa. 45:6).

Isaiah also prophesies about the feast that the King Himself will prepare for all people:

> And in this mountain the LORD of hosts will make for
> all people a feast of choice pieces, a feast of wines on
> the lees, of fat things full of marrow, of well-refined
> wines on the lees.
> —ISAIAH 25:6

The rule of God

The kingdom will be governed by our King. Isaiah prophesies this about the rule of God: "He will not fail nor be discouraged, till He has established justice in the earth; and the coastlands shall wait for His law" (Isa. 42:4). The rule of God will be known to all people by the King Himself.

> Listen to Me, My people; and give ear to Me, O My nation: for law will proceed from Me, and I will make My justice rest as a light of the peoples. My righteousness is near, My salvation has gone forth, and My arms will judge the peoples; the coastlands will wait upon Me, and on My arm they will trust.
>
> —ISAIAH 51:4–5

Isaiah encountered the glory of the Lord in the temple, and this glory would one day cover the earth as the waters covered the sea. One of the most encouraging words from Isaiah about life in the kingdom is this one: "For My house shall be called a house of prayer for all nations" (Isa. 56:7).

Israel would be restored through judgment and salvation. Judgment would come to the rebellious and salvation to the remnant (Isa. 1:9; 10:20–22; 11:16; 37:32). The remnant would be the foundation of the church, and the church would embrace the Gentiles. Christ's rule would come through judgment and salvation.

Israel is therefore glorified by the salvation of the Gentiles. Israel's influence, through their Messiah, becomes global. This would cause great rejoicing. (See Acts 15:3.)

JEREMIAH'S VISION OF THE KINGDOM

Jeremiah the priest was called to the prophetic office at a most unhappy time. Josiah's revival was over and its results short-lived. The final decline was under way. When the prophet was called, it was intimated that his message would be one of condemnation rather than of salvation. Throughout his long ministry of more than forty years, his preaching reflected this theme of judgment. God had risen early and sent His servants the prophets, but Israel would not hear. Now the fate predicted for an apostate nation in Deuteronomy 28–30 was inevitable. Babylon would capture Judah. And it would be best for the people to give in gracefully and so save their lives.

This message, coming to men whose desperate nationalism was all they had to cling to, was completely rejected, and Jeremiah was rejected with his message.[2]

Jeremiah was continually grieved at the apostasy of Israel. They were called to be God's people, but they were not living up to their calling. Jeremiah saw the day when Israel would be the people of God. Jeremiah's vision of the kingdom revealed the day when God's tabernacle would dwell in the midst of His people.

God wanted to dwell with man

God's original intent for Israel was to have a people to dwell among. When He gave the plans for the building of the tabernacle to Moses, He told Moses, "And let them make Me a sanctuary, that I may dwell among them" (Exod. 25:8).

But God was, and is, and always will be a holy God who will not tolerate sin. There was a condition for the Israelites to follow if they wanted to dwell in the presence of our holy God continually. Over and over again, He had to remind them of this condition.

> But this is what I commanded them, saying, "Obey
> My voice, and I will be your God, and you shall be
> My people. And walk in all the ways that I have com-
> manded you, that it may be well with you."
> —JEREMIAH 7:23

Finally, Israel's rebellion and apostasy caused God to say, "You are not My people, and I will not be your God" (Hosea 1:9).

Hosea then prophesied:

> Yet the number of the children of Israel shall be as
> the sand of the sea, which cannot be measured or

> numbered. And it shall come to pass in the place where
> it was said to them, "You are not My people," there it
> shall be said to them, "You are sons of the living God."
>
> —HOSEA 1:10

This became an important promise to the Jews. In the New Testament, Paul speaks of the expansion of the kingdom to the Gentiles, reminding the Jews of their rejection of Christ, quoting this passage in Hosea as now being fulfilled in Paul's day (Rom. 9:24–26). He concludes by saying, "What shall we say then? That Gentiles, who did not pursue righteousness, have attained to righteousness, even the righteousness of faith; but Israel, pursuing the law of righteousness, has not attained to the law of righteousness" (vv. 30–31).

God's restoration of Israel

In God's restoration of the Jews, God would give them a heart to know Him. This new heart would come through the new covenant. The Jews had broken the old covenant and so had come under the curse of God.

> Thus says the LORD God of Israel: "Cursed is the man
> who does not obey the words of this covenant which
> I commanded your fathers in the day I brought them
> out of the land of Egypt, from the iron furnace, saying,
> 'Obey My voice, and do according to all that I com-
> mand you; so shall you be My people, and I will be
> your God.'"
>
> —JEREMIAH 11:3–4

But with the new covenant would come a desire on the part of the people to love and serve God. This is the new creation, the new heart, the new spirit.

> For I will set My eyes on them for good, and I will
> bring them back to this land; I will build them and not
> pull them down, and I will plant them and not pluck
> them up. Then I will give them a heart to know Me,
> that I am the LORD; and they shall be My people, and I
> will be their God, for they shall return to Me with their
> whole heart.
>
> —JEREMIAH 24:6–7

The new covenant is one of the most important truths in
Jeremiah's prophecy. The new covenant would be the way God would
dwell among His people. The new covenant would open the way for
God to dwell in their midst through the new creation. With a new
heart, He would plant His law in their minds and hearts.

> But this is the covenant that I will make with the house
> of Israel after those days, says the LORD: I will put My
> law in their minds, and write it on their hearts; and I
> will be their God, and they shall be My people.
>
> —JEREMIAH 31:33

OTHER OLD TESTAMENT PROPHETS

There were many other Old Testament prophets, and many of them
also prophesied about the kingdom. These supported the prophecies
of Isaiah and Jeremiah.

The prophet Ezekiel also speaks of the new heart by saying:

> Then I will give them one heart, and I will put a new
> spirit within them, and take the stony heart out of their
> flesh, and give them a heart of flesh, that they may walk
> in My statutes and keep My judgments and do them;
> and they shall be My people, and I will be their God.
>
> —EZEKIEL 11:19–20

Ezekiel prophesied that God would set His tabernacle in their midst. His presence would dwell among them. God would give them a new heart and a new spirit. This again is the new creation, the arrival of the kingdom.

God has always desired to have a people. He desires to dwell among them and be their God: "My tabernacle also shall be with them; indeed I will be their God, and they shall be My people" (Ezek. 37:27). We are now the temple of God, and the Spirit of God dwells in us.

The prophet Zechariah prophesied of the expansion of the kingdom to the Gentile nations by saying:

> Many nations shall be joined to the LORD in that day, and they shall become My people. And I will dwell in your midst. Then you will know that the LORD of hosts has sent Me to you.
>
> —ZECHARIAH 2:11

God would also join many nations to Israel in that day. He would dwell in the midst of them. This is a prophecy about the church and the joining of the Jew and Gentile. This is a picture of the kingdom and God dwelling in the midst of the earth through Zion.

This is further confirmed by Paul in fulfillment of Hosea's prophecy. God would call the Gentiles, who had not been His people, to become a part of His people. He would be their God and dwell in their midst.

> What if God, wanting to show His wrath and to make His power known, endured with much longsuffering the vessels of wrath prepared for destruction, and that He might make known the riches of His glory on the vessels of mercy, which He had prepared beforehand for glory, even us whom He called, not of the Jews only,

but also of the Gentiles? As He says also in Hosea: "I will call them My people, who were not My people, and her beloved, who was not beloved." "And it shall come to pass in the place where it was said to them, 'You are not My people,' there they shall be called sons of the living God."

—ROMANS 9:22–26

God would also dwell among us through His ministry gifts, as prophesied in Psalm 68:18: "You have ascended on high, You have led captivity captive; You have received gifts among men, even from the rebellious, that the LORD God might dwell there." This refers to the church, as mentioned by Paul:

And He Himself gave some to be apostles, some prophets, some evangelists, and some pastors and teachers, for the equipping of the saints for the work of ministry, for the edifying of the body of Christ.

—EPHESIANS 4:11–12

CHAPTER 7

MANIFESTO OF THE KINGDOM

THE SERMON ON the Mount is the manifesto of the kingdom. According to the *Merriam-Webster Dictionary* online, a *manifesto* is a written statement declaring publicly the intentions, motives, or views of its issuer.[1] The Sermon on the Mount was a message for those who were hungering and thirsting for righteousness. They were waiting and expecting the *kingdom*. The kingdom was arriving, and those who entered were about to experience persecution from the religious elite of the day. The disciples were on the verge of witnessing the kingdom envisioned by the prophets. They would suffer persecution just as the prophets had. Jesus encouraged them to seek the kingdom and God's righteousness.

Jesus talked about the righteousness of the kingdom in the Sermon on the Mount (Matt. 5–7). The religious leaders of the day were outwardly righteous but inwardly wicked. The righteousness of the kingdom would exceed the righteousness of the Pharisees.

> Anyone who breaks one of the least of these commandments and teaches others to do the same will be called least in the kingdom of heaven, but whoever practices and teaches these commands will be called great in the kingdom of heaven. For I tell you that unless your righteousness surpasses that of the Pharisees and the teachers of the law, you will certainly not enter the kingdom of heaven.
>
> —MATTHEW 5:19–20, NIV

This righteousness would not be a legalistic righteousness but an inward righteousness produced by the Holy Spirit.

The Beatitudes, an integral part of the Sermon on the Mount, must be understood in the context of the kingdom. Jesus taught these truths as He was proclaiming the message of the kingdom. The Beatitudes were the blessings pronounced upon those who would participate in the kingdom. We will take a look at each of these to see what they say in the context of the kingdom.

KINGDOM FOR THE HUMBLE

> Blessed are the poor in spirit, for theirs is the kingdom of heaven.
>
> —MATTHEW 5:3, NIV

The poor in spirit would receive the kingdom. The Amplified Bible provides us with a definition of *the poor in spirit*: "the poor in spirit (the humble, who rate themselves insignificant)."

In Luke's version of the Beatitudes, this blessing is contrasted with the pronouncement of woe against the rich, who had already received their reward.

But woe to you who are rich, for you have received your consolation. Woe to you who are full, for you shall hunger. Woe to you who laugh now, for you shall mourn and weep.

—LUKE 6:24–25

The entire old-covenant world was about to be shaken and turned upside down with the arrival of the kingdom.

The poor in spirit are contrasted with the rich and proud. The full would be hungry, and those who laughed would mourn. The poor would be lifted and the high brought down. This understanding was not new to New Testament Jews. It is included in prophetic writings throughout the Old Testament. One example can be found in the song of Hannah, recorded in 1 Samuel:

He raises the poor from the dust and lifts the beggar from the ash heap, to set them among princes and make them inherit the throne of glory. For the pillars of the earth are the LORD's, and He has set the world upon them.

—1 SAMUEL 2:8

This is a law of the kingdom. God raises the poor out of the dust and sets them among princes and causes them to inherit the throne of glory. The poor go from a low place to ruling and reigning.

In Mary's song of exaltation, the Magnificat, she emphasizes the proud being made low:

He has put down the mighty from their thrones,
And exalted the lowly.
He has filled the hungry with good things,
And the rich He has sent away empty.

—LUKE 1:52–53

Those in positions of authority would lose their thrones, and those who had no power would rule and reign. The hungry would be filled, and the rich would suffer hunger. This is a total reversal of fortune.

KINGDOM OF COMFORT

Blessed are those who mourn, for they shall be comforted.
—MATTHEW 5:4

The arrival of the kingdom would bring an end to exile, defeat, mourning. It would bring comfort to those who mourned. The nation groaned under the burden of sin and bondage to the Romans. Their grief would be turned into joy at the arrival of the kingdom.

The arrival of the kingdom of God would amount to the end of the Jewish exile and thereby comfort the hearts of the mourners. The reason for their mourning would come to an end, and laughter would replace their tears. Luke's version of the Beatitudes says, "Blessed are you who weep now, for you shall laugh." The Old Testament spoke of a time when the Israelites' captivity was over, stating, "When the LORD brought back the captivity of Zion, we were like those who dream. Then our mouth was filled with laughter, and our tongue with singing" (Ps. 126:1).

The prophecies of Isaiah speak of a time when God would comfort His people. In Isaiah 40:1–3 we read:

"Comfort, yes, comfort My people!" says your God. "Speak comfort to Jerusalem, and cry out to her, that her warfare is ended, that her iniquity is pardoned; for she has received from the LORD's hand double for all her sins."

—ISAIAH 40:1–2

This is the promise of forgiveness of sin and the redemption that would come through Messiah. The time of punishment for sin was coming to an end. The result would be comfort for those who mourned under the bondage of sin and captivity.

Many were looking for the consolation of Israel. One example is Simeon. God had revealed to him that he would see the Messiah before he died. He had been led by the Spirit of God to come to Jerusalem and wait in the temple for the Christ to be revealed. It was there that he saw the baby Jesus soon after His birth. The Bible describes Simeon this way: "And behold, there was a man in Jerusalem whose name was Simeon, and this man was just and devout, waiting for the Consolation of Israel, and the Holy Spirit was upon him" (Luke 2:25).

Consolation is the comfort you feel when you are consoled in times of disappointment, thereby receiving relief from your grief. In this second Beatitude, comforting the mourners means nothing less than wiping away all tears from every eye, because sin and its curse have been taken away. Deliverance from the law of sin and death would mean an end of sorrow. (See Revelation 21:3–4; Isaiah 51:3–16; 65:17–19.)

The prophets saw the day when sorrow and mourning would flee away. Isaiah saw the day when comfort would come to those who mourned.

> So the ransomed of the LORD shall return, and come to
> Zion with singing, with everlasting joy on their heads.
> They shall obtain joy and gladness; sorrow and sighing
> shall flee away.
>
> —ISAIAH 51:11

Israel's days of mourning under captivity would end with the salvation provided by the Messiah. Joy would replace sorrow.

This was the hope of the kingdom, which was at hand when Jesus preached the gospel.

There are other references in Isaiah's prophecies to this day of comfort for God's people. Isaiah 65:19 speaks of the climate in Israel when this day arrives: "I will rejoice in Jerusalem, and joy in My people; the voice of weeping shall no longer be heard in her, nor the voice of crying." Isaiah recognized that it was the King Himself who would be the source of this rejoicing. The King would become the everlasting light in the kingdom, and there would be no need of the sun or moon. The days of mourning for the people would come to an end (Isa. 60:20).

Isaiah prophesied about the day that Israel would rise and shine because of Christ's light (Isa. 60:1). The nations (Gentiles) would come to the light, and the days of mourning would be ended.

> Those who sow in tears shall reap in joy.
> —PSALM 126:5

This promise is linked to the prophetic revelation of the end times in the Book of Revelation.

> For the Lamb who is in the midst of the throne will shepherd them and lead them to living fountains of waters. And God will wipe away every tear from their eyes.
> —REVELATION 7:17

> And God will wipe away every tear from their eyes; there shall be no more death, nor sorrow, nor crying. There shall be no more pain, for the former things have passed away.
> —REVELATION 21:4

KINGDOM FOR THE MEEK

Blessed are the meek, for they shall inherit the earth.
—MATTHEW 5:5

The meek (the mild, patient, long-suffering) would inherit the earth! The meek were the long-suffering. Jesus was quoting the promise of Psalm 37:11 when He stated this Beatitude: "The meek shall inherit the earth, and shall delight themselves in the abundance of peace."

This psalm is about the wicked prospering and the righteous waiting patiently for vindication. The arrival of the kingdom was the good news that justice was at hand. The wicked were about to be judged, and the meek were about to receive the inheritance of the kingdom.

The intended audience of Psalm 37 is the meek who watch the wicked prosper. The psalm advises the meek. These were the poor, powerless, and weak who found themselves oppressed by the wicked. The meek should not envy the apparent privileged position of the wicked.

The psalm promises that those with the self-control to wait patiently for God to bring about justice will receive a blessed inheritance of peace. Peace (or *shalom*) refers to the whole new created order—the kingdom of God. The psalm assures its readers that God will bring them into their promised inheritance of peace in its proper time. Meanwhile, remain patient. Do not attempt to force God's hand. Do not revert to violence. Be long-suffering and temperate, and God will give you the kingdom.

The psalm promises that those with the self-control to wait patiently for God to bring about justice will receive a blessed inheritance.

Do not fret because of evildoers,
Nor be envious of the workers of iniquity.
For they shall soon be cut down like the grass,
And wither as the green herb.
Trust in the LORD, and do good;

Dwell in the land, and feed on His faithfulness.
Delight yourself also in the LORD,
And He shall give you the desires of your heart.
Commit your way to the LORD,
Trust also in Him,
And He shall bring it to pass.
He shall bring forth your righteousness as the light,
And your justice as the noonday.
Rest in the LORD, and wait patiently for Him;
Do not fret because of him who prospers in his way,
Because of the man who brings wicked schemes to pass.
Cease from anger, and forsake wrath;
Do not fret—it only causes harm.
For evildoers shall be cut off;
But those who wait on the LORD,
They shall inherit the earth.
For yet a little while and the wicked shall be no more;
Indeed, you will look carefully for his place,
But it shall be no more.
But the meek shall inherit the earth,
And shall delight themselves in the abundance of peace.
—PSALM 37:1–11

The meek would inherit the kingdom. They would delight themselves in the abundance of peace (*shalom*). *Shalom* is peace, prosperity, health, and well-being. The psalm assures its readers that God will bring them into their promised inheritance of peace in its proper time. They must remain patient and not resort to violence. They would receive the kingdom by being long-suffering and patient.

Those who waited for the kingdom would rejoice in His salvation. The day of the kingdom would be a day of salvation. God would come and save: "And it will be said in that day: 'Behold, this is our

God; we have waited for Him, and He will save us. This is the LORD; we have waited for Him; we will be glad and rejoice in His salvation" (Isa. 25:9).

The King was coming to judge the oppressor and defend and deliver the meek. This was the hope of the meek. They believed that the Deliverer was coming. They put their trust in the Lord to bring the kingdom to the earth.

The meek would be rewarded for their trust and patience with an increase of joy (Isa. 29:19). The kingdom would bring joy for the meek and sorrow for the proud. The kingdom is a kingdom of joy and rejoicing.

The good news was preached to the meek.

> The Spirit of the Lord GOD is upon Me, because the LORD has anointed Me to preach good tidings to the poor; He has sent Me to heal the brokenhearted, to proclaim liberty to the captives, and the opening of the prison to those who are bound.
>
> —ISAIAH 61:1

They were waiting patiently for the gospel to come and received it with joy. They were waiting the arrival of the kingdom of God.

The meek would be hidden in the day of the Lord's anger. The Day of the Lord was at hand when Jesus announced the arrival of the kingdom. The Day of the Lord was a day of judgment. The meek would be saved, but the wicked would be judged (Zeph. 2:3).

The meek would be exalted to a high position in the kingdom, but the proud would be brought low.

> The LORD lifts up the humble; He casts the wicked down to the ground.
>
> —PSALM 147:6

This beatitude and the teachings related to it, like those in the Psalms, help believers to see the importance of living meek and humble lives.

> For the LORD takes pleasure in His people;
> He will beautify the humble with salvation.
>
> —PSALM 149:4

> Blessed are those who hunger and thirst for righteousness, for they shall be filled.
>
> —MATTHEW 5:6

SATISFACTION IN THE KINGDOM

Satisfaction from hunger and thirst is a picture of the kingdom. Psalm 22:26 tells us, "The poor shall eat and be satisfied." The poor would be filled, but the rich and proud would be sent away empty. In the Book of Luke we read, "He has filled the hungry with good things, and the rich He has sent away empty" (Luke 1:53).

Hunger is mentioned prophetically many times in the Old Testament. In Hannah's prophetic prayer, she alluded to the time when the full would be hungry and the hungry would be filled: "Those who were full have hired themselves out for bread, and the hungry have ceased to hunger" (1 Sam. 2:5).

Many times in the Bible *hunger* is symbolic of spiritual hunger. The Old Testament prophesied of the days when there would be a famine in the land, but not one of food.

> "Behold, the days are coming," says the Lord GOD,
> "That I will send a famine on the land, not a famine of
> bread, nor a thirst for water, but of hearing the words
> of the LORD. They shall wander from sea to sea, and
> from north to east; they shall run to and fro, seeking
> the word of the LORD, but shall not find it. In that day

the fair virgins and strong young men shall faint from thirst."

—AMOS 8:11–13

The kingdom is a place where the spiritual hunger in the hearts of people will be filled by the presence of our King. Psalm 107:9 states, "For He satisfies the longing soul, and fills the hungry soul with goodness." The wastelands and swamps that had been judged useless will suddenly spring forth into lush, new life.

He turns a wilderness into pools of water,
And dry land into watersprings.
There He makes the hungry dwell,
That they may establish a city for a dwelling place,
And sow fields and plant vineyards,
That they may yield a fruitful harvest.

—PSALM 107:35–37

Isaiah prophesied of the time when those who hunger and thirst for spiritual food would be filled. The presence of the King would fill the land with His presence: "They shall feed along the roads, and their pastures shall be on all desolate heights. They shall neither hunger nor thirst" (Isa. 49:9–10).

When Jesus walked on Earth, He often spoke about hunger and thirst. When He met the woman at the well of Samaria, He spoke to her about "living water." When she asked Him where she could get that living water, He told her, "Whoever drinks of this water will thirst again, but whoever drinks of the water that I shall give him will never thirst. But the water that I shall give him will become in him a fountain of water springing up into everlasting life" (John 4:13–14).

Shortly after He fed the five thousand with the five loaves and two fishes (John 6:1–14), He taught some of the people who had seen the miracle that they had seen only the material food and were satisfied in their physical lives, but they had not looked beyond the physical into the spiritual. He responds to their questions by contrasting food that perishes with food that endures unto eternal life.[2]

> Most assuredly, I say to you, you seek Me, not because you saw the signs, but because you ate of the loaves and were filled. Do not labor for the food which perishes, but for the food which endures to everlasting life, which the Son of Man will give you, because God the Father has set His seal on Him.
>
> —JOHN 6:26–27

Finally He revealed to them that He was the Bread they should seek. When they asked Him for the true bread from heaven, He said to them:

> I am the bread of life. He who comes to Me shall never hunger, and he who believes in Me shall never thirst.
>
> —JOHN 6:35

There would be no hunger and thirst in His kingdom, for He was the Bread of Life. If they longed for the spiritual food of righteousness, they would receive all they wanted.

When John the revelator is sharing his great vision of heaven in the Book of Revelation, he reveals what life in the kingdom is like for those who inherit eternal life with the King. He saw "a great multitude which no one could number, of all nations, tribes, peoples, and tongues, standing before the throne and before the Lamb, clothed with white robes, with palm branches in their hands, and crying out with a loud voice, saying, 'Salvation belongs to our God who sits on the throne, and to the Lamb!'" (Rev. 7:9–10). He describes who this great multitude is:

These are the ones who come out of the great tribulation, and washed their robes and made them white in the blood of the Lamb. Therefore they are before the throne of God, and serve Him day and night in His temple. And He who sits on the throne will dwell among them. They shall neither hunger anymore nor thirst anymore; the sun shall not strike them, nor any heat; for the Lamb who is in the midst of the throne will shepherd them and lead them to living fountains of waters. And God will wipe away every tear from their eyes.

—REVELATION 7:14–17

THE MERCIFUL KINGDOM

Blessed are the merciful, for they shall obtain mercy.
—MATTHEW 5:7

The kingdom would be a kingdom of mercy. The Old Testament prophecies spoke of a compassionate God: "But You, O Lord, are a God full of compassion, and gracious, longsuffering and abundant in mercy and truth" (Ps. 86:15).

The kingdom would have an open entrance for publicans and sinners. But the Pharisees—the spiritual leaders of the Jews—were legalistic and unmerciful. Jesus demonstrated the mercy of the kingdom by forgiving sins, healing the sick, cleansing lepers, healing lunatics, healing the blind, casting out demons, raising the dead, and feeding the multitudes (Matt. 14:14; 20:34). He had compassion and mercy on the poor, the diseased, and the outcasts of society. This was proof that the kingdom had arrived.

Jesus ministered with compassion. He called sinners to repentance. When John the Baptist came to Jesus and asked Him if He was, indeed, the Messiah, Jesus identified His works of mercy as proof that He was sent:

> Jesus answered and said to them, "Go and tell John the things which you hear and see: The blind see and the lame walk; the lepers are cleansed and the deaf hear; the dead are raised up and the poor have the gospel preached to them.
>
> —MATTHEW 11:4–5

God desired mercy rather than sacrifice. Religious observances are never a substitute for mercy. Religion without mercy is unacceptable to God: "For I desire mercy and not sacrifice, and the knowledge of God more than burnt offerings" (Hosea 6:6). Jesus demonstrated mercy and compassion.

The Pharisees had no mercy. They were legalistic and judgmental with sinners. They looked down upon people and did not lift one finger to help them. They did not understand the kingdom, and they did not understand the mercy mission of Christ. Jesus continually clashed with the Pharisees, and they rejected Him and His ministry.

> Now it happened, as Jesus sat at the table in the house, that behold, many tax collectors and sinners came and sat down with Him and His disciples. And when the Pharisees saw it, they said to His disciples, "Why does your Teacher eat with tax collectors and sinners?" When Jesus heard that, He said to them, "Those who are well have no need of a physician, but those who are sick. But go and learn what this means: 'I desire mercy and not sacrifice.' For I did not come to call the righteous, but sinners, to repentance."
>
> —MATTHEW 9:10–13

The prophets saw a coming kingdom of mercy. Micah's vision of the kingdom is one of mercy.

> "In that day," says the LORD, "I will assemble the
> lame, I will gather the outcast and those whom I have
> afflicted; I will make the lame a remnant, and the out-
> cast a strong nation; so the LORD will reign over them
> in Mount Zion from now on, even forever."
>
> —MICAH 4:6–7

The reign of God in Zion would be one of mercy. God would
bring in the afflicted and halted. The lame would leap and the dumb
would sing (Isa. 35:6). The outcasts of society would be welcomed in the
kingdom. These are prophecies that connect the mercy of God to the
kingdom. Jesus fulfilled these prophecies, thereby revealing Himself
as the King of the kingdom of heaven for all who would believe (Matt.
15:30). Multitudes were healed. The lame, blind, and dumb were healed.
This reveals the mercy and compassion of Christ and His kingdom.

Micah's prophecies emphasized justice, mercy, and humility, as
opposed to sacrifices. Micah's prophecies play a key role throughout
the Book of Matthew, which emphasizes the kingdom of heaven.
By extending mercy to society's least desirable people, Jesus offers a
vision of God's kingdom that differed markedly from the prevailing
schools of thought and practice offered by the Pharisees.

The Pharisees were more concerned with the external require-
ments of the Torah than with the needs of the sheep. The condition
of the sheep revealed the failure of the leaders who were responsible
to watch for and protect them.

> Then Jesus went about all the cities and villages,
> teaching in their synagogues, preaching the gospel of the
> kingdom, and healing every sickness and every disease
> among the people. But when He saw the multitudes, He
> was moved with compassion for them, because they were
> weary and scattered, like sheep having no shepherd.
>
> —MATTHEW 9:35–36

The New International Version says they were "harassed and helpless, like sheep without a shepherd." The Amplified Bible says in verse 36, "When He saw the throngs, He was moved with pity and sympathy for them, because they were bewildered (harassed and distressed and dejected and helpless), like sheep without a shepherd." When Jesus saw the multitudes and their condition, He was moved with compassion. Jesus then sent out the Twelve and the Seventy to meet the needs of the sheep.

THE PURE IN HEART

> Blessed are the pure in heart, for they shall see God.
> —MATTHEW 5:8

The pure in heart are the clean in heart. In Old Testament times, those with clean hearts were troubled by the prosperity of the wicked.

> Truly God is good to Israel,
> To such as are pure in heart.
> But as for me, my feet had almost stumbled;
> My steps had nearly slipped.
> For I was envious of the boastful,
> When I saw the prosperity of the wicked.
> —PSALM 73:1–3

Psalm 73 is a psalm that echoes the complaint of the clean in heart at the prosperity of the wicked. The pure in heart were about to see the arrival of the kingdom and judgment upon the wicked.

Compare the prosperity of the wicked with the suffering of the righteous at the time of the kingdom's arrival. But the tables were about to be turned. The kingdom meant vindication for the righteous and judgment for the wicked. The pure in heart would ascend to the hill of the Lord (Zion). The pure in heart would inherit the kingdom.

This was the opposite of the religious leaders of the day. The Pharisees were preoccupied with ceremonial cleansing, but the kingdom would emphasize the cleansing of the heart. Jesus rebuked the Pharisees: "Blind Pharisee, first cleanse the inside of the cup and dish, that the outside of them may be clean also" (Matt. 23:26). Ceremonial cleansing would not produce the kingdom. The religious leaders who emphasized ceremonial cleansing but not inward cleansing would not see God or His kingdom.

The religious leaders in Israel could not speak good things because their hearts were unclean. They accused Christ of casting out devils by Beelzebub. When He healed the paralytic, they accused Him of blasphemy (Matt. 9:3).

The kingdom came and exposed what was in the hearts of men. The evil in the heart was exposed by the preaching and demonstration of the kingdom. Many did not enter the kingdom because of the condition of their heart. Jesus "looked around at them with anger, being grieved by the hardness of their hearts" (Mark 3:5). He confronted them with their evil, pointing out to them that God saw their hearts.

> And He said to them, "You are those who justify yourselves before men, but God knows your hearts. For what is highly esteemed among men is an abomination in the sight of God."
>
> —LUKE 16:15

God wants His kingdom to be filled with people who are pure in heart. Paul supported this desire by telling early Christians:

> Since you have purified your souls in obeying the truth through the Spirit in sincere love of the brethren, love one another fervently with a pure heart, having been

born again, not of corruptible seed but incorruptible, through the word of God which lives and abides forever.

—1 PETER 1:22–23

A KINGDOM OF PEACE

Blessed are the peacemakers, for they shall be called sons of God.

—MATTHEW 5:9

The kingdom is for the peacemakers. Peacemakers are those who enjoy peace and strive for peace. The wicked hate peace and love war.

Those who make peace are the opposite of those who make war. The peacemakers would inherit the kingdom and be called the children of God. The proud and violent would not enter the kingdom but would be judged. The peacemakers were the meek, the pure in heart. The peacemakers were the righteous waiting for deliverance from the wicked, who delighted in war (Ps. 140:2–3).

The Pharisees were for war. They sought to destroy Christ. They persecuted Christ and His followers. They were not peacemakers. They would not inherit the kingdom. They were murderers. They were violent. This struggle between the wicked and the righteous was coming to a close at the end of Israel's age. The righteous would triumph in their King.

The Pharisees continually plotted to destroy Christ. When He healed the man with a withered hand on the Sabbath, they "went out and immediately held a consultation with the Herodians against Him, how they might [devise some means to] put Him to death" (Mark 3:6, AMP). After Jesus raised Lazarus from the dead, the Pharisees also wanted to put Lazarus to death (John 12:10).

These were violent, wicked men. They would have no place in the kingdom. They would be cast out, while others came from the uttermost part of the earth to enter the kingdom. The kingdom is not for the proud and the violent. The kingdom is for the peacemakers.

The meek, the humble, and the peacemakers would be redeemed from violence. The cry of the righteous would be heard. God would not leave them in the hands of the violent.

> He will redeem their life from oppression and violence;
> And precious shall be their blood in His sight.
> —PSALM 72:14

The kingdom is a kingdom of peace, and citizens of the kingdom are peacemakers. This is what the prophets envisioned, and Christ was proclaiming the time was near.

> For thus says the LORD: "Behold, I will extend peace to her like a river, and the glory of the Gentiles like a flowing stream. Then you shall feed; on her sides shall you be carried, and be dandled on her knees. As one whom his mother comforts, so I will comfort you; and you shall be comforted in Jerusalem."
> —ISAIAH 66:12–13

The meek, humble, and pure would enjoy the peace of the kingdom. They would be delivered from strife and violence. Their Redeemer had come. The good news had arrived. God had kept His promise.

But although the good news had arrived, many who had the opportunity to recognize Jesus as the King who was ushering in the kingdom failed to do so. Jesus wept over the city of Jerusalem because the peace of God was hidden from their eyes. Jerusalem would not experience peace but judgment. More than anyone else, He understood what would be the consequences of their rejection.

> Now as He drew near, He saw the city and wept over it, saying, "If you had known, even you, especially in this

your day, the things that make for your peace! But now they are hidden from your eyes. For days will come upon you when your enemies will build an embankment around you, surround you and close you in on every side, and level you, and your children within you, to the ground; and they will not leave in you one stone upon another, because you did not know the time of your visitation."

—LUKE 19:41–44

But the peacemakers would be called the children of God.

A PERSECUTED KINGDOM

Blessed are those who are persecuted for righteousness' sake, for theirs is the kingdom of heaven. Blessed are you when they revile and persecute you, and say all kinds of evil against you falsely for My sake. Rejoice and be exceedingly glad, for great is your reward in heaven, for so they persecuted the prophets who were before you.

—MATTHEW 5:10–12

The disciples were on the verge of witnessing the kingdom envisioned by the prophets. They would suffer persecution, just as the prophets had. They would suffer persecution from the elites, who had the incorrect view of the kingdom.

When Stephen rebuked Israel for their mistreatment of the prophets, as well as their mistreatment of the new-covenant believers, he was persecuted and killed (Acts 7). But although Stephen was persecuted and killed, he was blessed by God and received his eternal reward.

The Jews did not understand that entrance into the kingdom would involve persecution. Many who heard the word of the kingdom were offended because of persecution. These were those who received the word in stony places.

> But he who received the seed on stony places, this is he
> who hears the word and immediately receives it with
> joy; yet he has no root in himself, but endures only
> for a while. For when tribulation or persecution arises
> because of the word, immediately he stumbles.
> —MATTHEW 13:20–21

Jesus understood that His ministry announced the fulfillment of the Old Testament prophecies. He taught His followers that those who followed Him would face persecution for the sake of righteousness. But eventually they would experience the blessing of receiving the kingdom in all of its fullness.

The kingdom was at hand, many were entering, and many would suffer for doing the will of the Father. Those who connected to the King would also connect to His suffering. Peter affirmed this in his letter to the early believers.

> But sanctify the Lord God in your hearts, and always
> be ready to give a defense to everyone who asks you a
> reason for the hope that is in you, with meekness and
> fear; having a good conscience, that when they defame
> you as evildoers, those who revile your good conduct in
> Christ may be ashamed. For it is better, if it is the will
> of God, to suffer for doing good than for doing evil.
> —1 PETER 3:15–17

Jesus attacked the hardness of men's hearts in putting away their wives. The Pharisees allowed divorce at the whim of men. Men were guilty of adultery by putting away their wives and remarrying for no scriptural reason. The Pharisees were teaching men to break the commandments through their traditions. They would be least in the kingdom.

When the kingdom arrived, people were concerned about life

and the future. Jesus makes seeking the kingdom a priority. The kingdom would make all things needed available. The same is true today. Those who discover and enter the kingdom begin a life of faith. The life of faith eliminates worry concerning the future. Those outside the kingdom are filled with worry and stress.

Those who did not make the kingdom a priority were in danger of missing it. Many have missed the kingdom through the ages. To miss the opportunity of the kingdom is tragic.

The kingdom must be a priority. You cannot afford to be apathetic when it comes to the kingdom. The kingdom is blessed, and there are great blessings to those who live and walk in the kingdom. The kingdom must become a lifestyle.

Christ is blessed forever and worthy of our worship (Ps. 45:2). The kingdom is blessed. The King is blessed. The citizens of the kingdom are blessed. Those who apprehend the kingdom will be blessed.

I encourage those who read this book to meditate upon the truths presented here. I believe these truths can change your life. The kingdom is inexhaustible. There is no limit to the depth of and height of the kingdom. There is so much to learn from the Scriptures concerning the kingdom. It is the glory of God to conceal a thing, and it is the honor of kings to search out a matter. The mysteries of the kingdom can be revealed to you. You can walk in the blessing of revelation. Jesus said:

> For I tell you that many prophets and kings have desired to see what you see, and have not seen it, and to hear what you hear, and have not heard it.
>
> —LUKE 10:24

We have the privilege of understanding the kingdom and receiving its blessing. Don't allow anything to keep you from the kingdom and its kingdom blessings.

CHAPTER 8

THE CHURCH AND THE KINGDOM

THE KINGDOM IS a mystery. The Jews could not understand it unless the understanding was given. Jesus told His followers, "To you it has been given to know the mysteries of the kingdom of God, but to the rest it is given in parables that 'seeing they may not see, and hearing they may not understand'" (Luke 8:10).

Paul talked about the mysteries revealed to him. Like the kingdom, the establishment of the church was a mystery. The mystery of the kingdom is that God would rule over His new-creation people, the church. The mystery is in Christ. We are those who are in Christ.

What did come to pass was the establishment of new-covenant people, called the church. This was a completely new community consisting of both Jews and Gentiles in Christ. It was a mystery that had been hidden from previous ages and generations, but it was revealed to the apostles and prophets by the Spirit. The church is a manifestation of the kingdom. It was not earthly or carnal but heavenly and spiritual. The saints were called to live in the Spirit, and they were seated in heavenly places in Christ. They served an invisible King.

He was, is, and will always be the King of saints. Saints are holy ones. The saints were promised the kingdom. Daniel 7:18 tells us, "The saints of the Most High shall receive the kingdom, and possess the kingdom forever, even forever and ever." The saints are those who are in Christ. Therefore the church—the *called-out ones* (saints)—are those who possess the kingdom.

During the time of Christ, not everyone possessed the kingdom of God. The only ones who did were those who received Christ by faith. Those who rejected Him could not enter into Him. If you are not in Christ, you are not a saint. Being a saint has nothing to do with *your* works; it's all about *His* work. It is gained entirely by grace through faith.

The church is the eternal purpose of God. The kingdom is eternal, and the church is eternal. This was God's eternal purpose from the foundation of the world, as we can see in Ephesians 1:4: "He chose us in Him before the foundation of the world, that we should be holy and without blame before Him in love." We are an "eternal excellence," the joy of many generations (Isa. 60:15). This excellence (glory) is in the church from generation to generation and age to age (Eph. 3:21). This is the kingdom, the church age, the age of glory. The kingdom of God is glorious!

> For the earth will be filled with the knowledge of the glory of the LORD, as the waters cover the sea.
> —HABAKKUK 2:14

The mystery of the kingdom and church was revealed to Paul. He admonished the Thessalonians to "walk worthy of God who calls you into His own kingdom and glory" (1 Thess. 2:12). He told the church at Ephesus that God had revealed the mystery of the kingdom to him "to the intent that now the manifold wisdom of God might be made known by the church…according to the eternal purpose which He accomplished in Christ Jesus our Lord" (Eph. 3:10–11).

The Gentiles would be fellow heirs with the Jews. The church was the goal of the ages. The arrival of the kingdom meant the arrival of the church.

> For we are His workmanship, created in Christ Jesus for good works, which God prepared beforehand that we should walk in them.
>
> —EPHESIANS 2:10

"We are His workmanship, created in Christ Jesus." We are the saints, the possessors of the kingdom, the new creation, Zion. God has created us to do good works.

THE ADVANCEMENT OF THE KINGDOM

The kingdom is not being *established*. It is being *advanced*. It *was established* in the days of the Roman kings.

> And in the days of these kings the God of heaven will set up a kingdom which shall never be destroyed; and the kingdom shall not be left to other people; it shall break in pieces and consume all these kingdoms, and it shall stand forever.
>
> —DANIEL 2:44

The kingdom is being advanced from generation to generation through preaching, teaching, healing, deliverance, praise, prayer, worship, and prophesying. There are more believers on Earth today than at any time in history. In Luke 10:11 we read, "The very dust of your city which clings to us we wipe off against you. Nevertheless know this, that the kingdom of God has come near you."

The kingdom came—*nevertheless. Nevertheless* means "despite anything to the contrary, notwithstanding, all the same, in spite of." In other words, the kingdom came in spite of the opposition of many. The kingdom was not postponed because of the unbelief or opposition of many.

THE CHURCH IS THE
AGENT OF THE KINGDOM

The church is the agent of the kingdom. An agent is "one who acts or has the power or authority to act, one empowered to act for or represent another: an author's agent; an insurance agent. A means by which something is done or caused; instrument. A force or substance that causes a change: a chemical agent; an infectious agent."

The church is the visible representative of the invisible King and His kingdom. The church is the embassy of the kingdom, and the saints are the ambassadors of the kingdom. An *ambassador* is "a diplomatic agent of the highest rank accredited to a foreign government or sovereign as the resident representative of his or her own government for a special and often temporary diplomatic assignment; an authorized representative or messenger."[1] We represent the government of heaven.

As ambassadors, we are delegates of the kingdom. We have been given power and authority to advance the kingdom. "Now then, we are ambassadors for Christ, as though God were pleading through us: we implore you on Christ's behalf, be reconciled to God" (2 Cor. 5:20).

Every king and kingdom has ambassadors and delegates sent to conduct the affairs of the king. The heavenly kingdom is no exception. God sends people in every generation to conduct the affairs of His kingdom. We are responsible to be faithful in fulfilling our commissions.

To reject the King's ambassadors is to reject the King: "He who receives you receives Me, and he who receives Me receives Him who sent Me" (Matt. 10:40). The sent one represents the Sender. The apostles were sent by Jesus with power and authority to preach and demonstrate the kingdom. They were the legal representatives of the Sender. Those who granted them hospitality would be blessed, and those who mistreated them would be judged. They were sent to preach the good news of the kingdom, the rule and reign of God. Those who despised the message despised the rule and reign of God.

The apostles are likened to the prophets who were sent to disobedient Israel. The prophets represented the heavenly King who had a covenant relationship with Israel. The prophets were sent to speak the King's words and warn Israel of their covenant violations. Those who mistreated the prophets were judged, and those who blessed the prophets were rewarded.

> He who receives a prophet in the name of a prophet
> shall receive a prophet's reward. And he who receives
> a righteous man in the name of a righteous man shall
> receive a righteous man's reward.
> —MATTHEW 10:41

In Matthew 22 we find the parable of the wedding feast. In it, Jesus talks about the man who sent his servants out to invite people to the marriage of his son. However, some of his servants were mistreated, and others were killed by those the man was attempting to invite to the wedding.

> Tell those who are invited, "See, I have prepared my
> dinner; my oxen and fatted cattle are killed, and all
> things are ready. Come to the wedding." But they made

> light of it and went their ways, one to his own farm, another to his business. And the rest seized his servants, treated them spitefully, and killed them. But when the king heard about it, he was furious. And he sent out his armies, destroyed those murderers, and burned up their city.
>
> —MATTHEW 22:4–8

The king was very angry because his servants were mistreated. Those who mistreated these servants are symbolic of the nation of Israel and its treatment of God's Son, Jesus.

In the parable, as a result of their mistreatment, the king sent forth his armies and burned the city where they lived. The city of Jerusalem was burned with fire by Titus and the Romans in A.D. 70. The old covenant city had rejected the rule of the King. The old covenant city was guilty of murder, and the King executed judgment.

The church is, and has been, the purpose of God from the foundation of the world. The mystery of the church was revealed to Paul. The creation of a new people in Christ was a mystery hidden in previous ages.

WORLD WITHOUT END

The kingdom is from generation to generation, and the church is from generation to generation. The church is eternal and the kingdom is eternal: "To Him be glory in the church by Christ Jesus to all generations, forever and ever" (Eph. 3:21).

The kingdom would bring everlasting salvation "world without end."

> But Israel shall be saved in the LORD with an everlasting salvation: ye shall not be ashamed nor confounded world without end.
>
> —ISAIAH 45:17, KJV

Israel's salvation is "world without end," and there is glory in the church "world without end." God joined the Gentiles to Israel's salvation and formed the church. This is the kingdom of God "world without end."

> One generation shall praise Your works to another,
> And shall declare Your mighty acts.
>
> —Psalm 145:4

> The Lord shall reign forever—
> Your God, O Zion, to all generations.
> Praise the Lord!
>
> —Psalm 146:10

These verses emphasize the eternal aspect of the kingdom (from generation to generation). Zion is from generation to generation. Each generation praises God's mighty works, and the mighty acts of God are seen in every generation.

The church was the goal of the ages. Jesus came at the end of the world (literally, "the consummation of the ages") to establish the church and the kingdom. The increase of the kingdom has no end.

> For then would He often have had to suffer [over and over again] since the foundation of the world. But as it now is, He has once for all at the consummation and close of the ages appeared to put away and abolish sin by His sacrifice [of Himself].
>
> —Hebrews 9:26, AMP

Jesus came to establish the kingdom at the end of the old-covenant age. He came in the fullness of time to end the old and establish the new. This was God's plan from the foundation of the world. What had been a mystery was now revealed. The Old Testament types became realities in Christ.

The kingdom of God is not about holy days or holy seasons. Colossians 2:16–17 says, "So let no one judge you in food or in drink, or regarding a festival or a new moon or sabbaths, which are a shadow of things to come, but the substance is of Christ." It is not about a holy land. The old-covenant holy days and land were simply earthly types of Christ. The kingdom is not about whether you worship on Saturday or Sunday. It is not about Jewish holy days. There is liberty in the kingdom. Legalism and bondage have no place in the kingdom.

The kingdom is not carnal. It is not meat and drink: "For the kingdom of God is not eating and drinking, but righteousness and peace and joy in the Holy Spirit" (Rom. 14:17). The kingdom is not based on what you eat or don't eat. This is one of the hardest things for some to learn. People still try to make the kingdom about eating and drinking. The old-covenant ordinances of eating do not apply in the kingdom age. These Old Testament examples stand as types of unclean people. God told Peter to kill and eat. The Old Testament types of the kingdom are now realities in Christ. Those who want a physical, observable kingdom get caught up in physical, carnal things.

Jesus talked about spiritual meat, and Paul talked about spiritual drink. You must eat the flesh of the Son of man and drink His blood. Many of Christ's followers no longer walked with Him after He taught these truths about the kingdom, teaching instead that *spiritual food* and *spiritual drink* are what matter in the kingdom.

The kingdom is not about Jew or Gentile, male or female, bond or free. All people, regardless of background, gender, or social status, have access to the kingdom through faith in Christ.

There is no racism or prejudice in the kingdom. These things are fleshly and have no place in the kingdom. In Christ there is neither Jew nor Gentile. The kingdom breaks down racial barriers. This is what happened in the early church, and it has happened throughout history. It happened at Azusa Street at the turn of the twentieth century when blacks and whites worshiped together during a time in the world when there was intense prejudice and racism prevalent.

The kingdom is not racial because it is not fleshly. The kingdom does not exalt one group or people or one person over another. The Holy Spirit, when allowed free course, will always break down racial and cultural barriers. The greatest barrier that was broken was between Jew and Gentile.

Pride of race, culture, background, and gender have no place in the kingdom. Humility is a hallmark of the kingdom. God has no respect of persons (Acts 10:34, KJV).

KINGDOM KEYS

The keys of the kingdom were given to Peter based on his revelation that Jesus was the Christ, the Son of God. Jesus built His church upon this rock—the revelation of Christ (Matt. 16:18). This verse connects the kingdom with the church. Peter was used by God to open the kingdom to the Jews at Pentecost and to the Gentiles in the house of Cornelius.

If the kingdom was to be postponed, why would Jesus give the keys of the kingdom? Keys are meant to be used to open and to close. The authority of the kingdom was released with the arrival of the kingdom. There is no such thing as a kingdom with no power and authority.

The keys of the kingdom represent the authority of the kingdom. Keys give access. Keys open and lock doors. The authority of the kingdom was given to Peter because of a revelation. Those who have this revelation have authority. The authority of the kingdom is based on revelation. Those who walk in kingdom power and authority are those who have revelation.

The church possesses the revelation of the plans and purposes of God. Paul prayed for the saints to have a spirit of wisdom and revelation. He prayed for the eyes of their understanding to be enlightened. He desired the church to understand the mysteries of the kingdom. He preached and taught the mystery of Christ that was revealed to him by the Spirit. His revelation of the church is critical. (See Ephesians 1:15–23.)

The mystery of the kingdom has been revealed. That which was hidden in previous ages has been revealed. Christ is the end of the Law. Christ and His body were the goal. Christ and His kingdom were the goal. The rule of Christ over His people was the goal.

The new creation is the new circumcision. We are the people of God, circumcised in the heart. The circumcision of the flesh was a covenant sign, a type. The circumcision of the heart is the antitype. (See Colossians 2:11–15.)

It is important to note that sometimes the local church is not synonymous with the kingdom. There are churches where Satan has a large measure of effective control. The will of God is not done in these churches. This is evidenced not only by false doctrine but also by a lack of love and the presence of all kinds of relational and personal sin. Strife, division, carnality, and rampant sin are not the marks of the kingdom.

The visible, organizational church has often exhibited the opposite of righteousness, peace, and joy in the Holy Ghost. There are many churches that deny the power of God and the anointing of the Holy Spirit. The church has often been sectarian. The kingdom goes beyond denomination and sects. We cannot be confused in this area. God's kingdom is holy, and His people are called to be holy.

C. Peter Wagner states:

> Over the years, many institutional forms of the Christian Church have evolved that are far from what Jesus had in mind as He was instructing His disciples.

Without naming names, it is a fact that all too much of
what is known as Christianity is actively promulgating
deeds and words that are quite different from what we
know of the kingdom of God, and are not a reflection of
God's will in the world today. Such so-called "churches"
are not to be identified with the kingdom of God. But,
at the same time, multitudes of churches in many parts
of the world, although imperfectly, do accurately reflect
the glory of God through Jesus Christ and, as such, can
be considered outposts of the kingdom of God.[2]

The kingdom of God is heavenly and spiritual, not earthly and
carnal. Earthly organizations, even Christian ones, are not neces-
sarily the representatives of the kingdom of God. The true church
has come to heavenly Zion. The true church will manifest righteousness, peace, and joy in the Holy Ghost. The church should be a manifestation of the kingdom of God. The church is intended to be salt
and light. It should represent heaven on Earth.

The church should be a kingdom community of believers
serving one another in love and humility.

And whosoever of you will be the chiefest, shall be servant of all.

—MARK 10:44, KJV

For you, brethren, have been called to liberty; only
do not use liberty as an opportunity for the flesh, but
through love serve one another.

—GALATIANS 5:13

Service is the hallmark of the kingdom. When believers do not
serve one another but serve themselves instead, it is no longer reflective of the kingdom. When the church no longer *serves* but instead
exists to *be served*, it is no longer reflective of the kingdom. When

leaders no longer serve but demand to be served, they no longer reflect either the heart of the King or the characteristics of the kingdom.

> For even the Son of Man did not come to be served, but to serve, and to give His life a ransom for many.
>
> —MARK 10:45

God calls Jesus, the Messiah, "My Servant" (Isa. 42:1; 52:13). God's individual "Servant" would accomplish what the national *servant* (Israel) could not. We are now servants in Christ. The Servant would suffer and "sprinkle many nations" (Isa. 52:15). The verse continues by saying, "For what had not been told them they shall see, and what they had not heard they shall consider." This verse was quoted by Paul in Romans 15:21, which is the fulfillment of the prophecy by Isaiah being preached to Gentiles.

In the kingdom we are to be submitted to one another under the reign of Christ.

> Likewise you younger people, submit yourselves to your elders. Yes, all of you be submissive to one another, and be clothed with humility, for "God resists the proud, but gives grace to the humble."
>
> —1 PETER 5:5

Too often Christians do not serve and submit to one another but instead walk in strife and division. Again, this is not reflective of the kingdom.

The kingdom of God has often been called *the upside-down kingdom*. In the kingdom, the way *up* is *down*. It is the opposite of this in the kingdoms of the world, which are often characterized by everyone trying to get to the top. Selfish ambition and pride have no place in the kingdom of God.

John the Baptist quoted Isaiah to prophesy Jesus's arrival: "Every valley shall be filled and every mountain and hill brought low; the crooked places shall be made straight and the rough ways smooth" (Luke 3:5). Mountains (the proud) are brought low in the kingdom. Valleys (the low) are filled (made high) in the kingdom. Everything is turned upside down.

Jesus teaches that the first are made last, and the last are made first (Matt. 19:30). The proud are humbled, and the humble are exalted (Matt. 23:11–12). Once again everything is turned upside down. This is what happened when the kingdom came. The old-covenant world was turned upside down. The new-covenant world came into being.

Jesus uses a child to symbolize the kingdom:

> Therefore whoever humbles himself as this little child is
> the greatest in the kingdom of heaven.
> —MATTHEW 18:4

Children rank low in status and power; they are dependent. Becoming like a child is the key to being great in the kingdom. We are called to serve rather than to seek power. Jesus is our example. He humbled Himself, took on the form of a servant, and became obedient to the death of the cross (Phil. 2:8). He is now highly exalted and given a name above every name.

CHAPTER 9

GROWTH AND ADVANCEMENT
OF THE KINGDOM

T HE BOOK OF Acts is a continuation of what Jesus began to do and teach. Jesus began preaching, teaching, and demonstrating the kingdom. The kingdom message and demonstration would now *continue* through the apostles and the church.

> The former account I made, O Theophilus, of all that
> Jesus began both to do and teach.
> —ACTS 1:1

Throughout the Book of Acts (as well as in several other places), we see the importance of speaking about and proclaiming the kingdom of God. (See Acts 1:6; 8:12; 14:22; 19:8; 20:25.) Furthermore, we see that this type of proclamation is a continuation of what Jesus was doing and that the proclamation was unhindered even when the one proclaiming was imprisoned.

Alan Knox explains:

> It seems, then, that Luke intended his second volume to be a treatise on the expansion of the kingdom of God. However, Luke did not intend Acts to be a treatise on the beginning of the kingdom. His gospel explained that Jesus was the beginning of the kingdom of God. Similarly, Luke did not intend Acts to be a treatise on the end of the expansion of the kingdom. Instead, the kingdom continues to be proclaimed at the end of the book.[1]

The Book of Acts shows us that the kingdom is not some theological concept but a living reality in the lives of people. People are dramatically transformed by the power and message of the kingdom. The Book of Acts is a book of *action*, which shows us that God is actively involved with His church in advancing the kingdom. This happens through miracles, healings, angels, visions, judgments, and prayer.

EXPANSION OF THE KINGDOM

In Psalm 2:1, the *heathen* are identified as "the nations," or the world. In the time of the writing of the psalms, the world was divided into "Hebrew nations" and "other nations"—the people of God and foreigners. The same division is often referred to in the New Testament under the terms *Jew* and *Gentile*, because the Greeks divided all the world into "Greeks" and "barbarians." The world now embraces all the nations that are not under the influence of the true religion.

> But you shall receive power when the Holy Spirit has come upon you; and you shall be witnesses to Me in

Jerusalem, and in all Judea and Samaria, and to the end of the earth.

—ACTS 1:8

The expansion of the kingdom is one of the themes of the Book of Acts. The kingdom would expand from Jerusalem to "the uttermost part of the earth" (Acts 1:8, KJV). In Albert Barnes's *Barnes's Notes on the New Testament*, he explains, "The uttermost parts of the earth were the farthest regions of the world. This promise would properly embrace all the world as then known, as it is now known, as it shall be hereafter known."[2]

Ask of me, and I shall give thee the heathen for thine inheritance, and the uttermost parts of the earth for thy possession.

—PSALM 2:8, KJV

By "the Heathen," and "the uttermost parts of the earth," are meant God's elect among the Gentiles, and who live in the distant parts of the world; which are Christ's other sheep, the Father has given to him as his portion, and whom he has made his care and charge: as if it was not enough that he should be King of Zion, or have the government over his chosen ones among the Jews, he commits into his hands the Gentiles also; see Isaiah 49:6; and these are given him as his inheritance and possession, as his portion, to be enjoyed by him; and who esteems them as such, and reckons them a goodly heritage, and a peculiar treasure, his jewels, and the apple of his eye. These words respect the calling of the Gentiles under the Gospel dispensation; and the amplitude of Christ's kingdom in all the earth, which shall be from sea to sea, and from the rivers to the ends of the earth.[3]

The blessing of salvation came upon Israel first and then went to the uttermost part of the earth (Ps. 67:7). Salvation was proclaimed in Jerusalem first and then preached to all nations.

In Psalm 72:8, David prayed for his son Solomon, saying, "He shall have dominion also from sea to sea, and from the River to the ends of the earth." Solomon's reign over the land was a type of Christ's dominion over the earth. The dominion of Christ would come through the gospel.

David and others prophesied often in the Psalms about the whole earth experiencing salvation. These were prophecies about the kingdom. David, who was a king, prophesied often about the greater kingdom of his Seed, Christ, the Messiah. Some of those prophecies in the Book of Psalms are shown below:

- "You are My Son...I will give You the nations for Your inheritance" (Ps. 2:7–8).

- "All the families of the nations shall worship before You" (Ps. 22:27).

- "The earth is the LORD's" (Ps. 24:1).

- "According to Your name, O God, so is Your praise to the ends of the earth" (Ps. 48:10).

- "You who are the confidence of all the ends of the earth" (Ps. 65:5).

- "All nations whom You have made shall come and worship before you, O Lord" (Ps. 86:10).

- "The nations shall fear the name of the LORD, and all the kings of the earth Your glory" (Ps. 102:15).

- "Be exalted, O God, above the heavens, and Your glory above all the earth" (Ps. 108:5).

The vision of the prophets was always global. The kingdom would not be limited to Palestine but would encompass all nations. The scribes and teachers understood this but did not understand how it would be accomplished. It would come through the death of the Messiah and the preaching of the gospel.

When reading these scriptures there should be no doubt of the plan and purpose of God. This purpose comes through the church, the new-creation people, who will become a global phenomenon. The church could not be limited to Jerusalem. The Book of Acts is the story of the church and kingdom breaking out of the framework of the old covenant and breaking forth throughout the earth. What began as a small sect of Nazarenes became a global movement that could not be stopped.

The Book of Acts is therefore the fulfillment of the prophecy that the kingdom would extend to the uttermost parts of the earth. The book begins with Jesus speaking of the kingdom and ends with Paul at Rome speaking of the kingdom.

Before Acts was written, the kingdom message was only preached to Israel. Jesus told the twelve disciples to only go to "the lost sheep of the house of Israel" (Matt. 10:6). They were forbidden by Jesus to go into the way of the Gentiles or Samaritans. The kingdom message was to be given to the Jew first. This was because God could not bring salvation to the nations until He brought salvation to Israel and fulfilled His promise to them.

Stephen, the first martyr, seemed to have a better understanding of the kingdom than many had in his day. His words cut to the heart of unbelieving Israel.

> But Solomon built Him a house. However, the Most High does not dwell in temples made with hands, as the prophet says: "Heaven is My throne, and earth is

> My footstool. What house will you build for Me? says
> the LORD, or what is the place of My rest?"
>
> —ACTS 7:47–49

Stephen understood that God's presence could not be limited
to a temple. The temple was only a temporary resting place until
God formed a people to dwell among. He recounted Israel's historical rebellion. The judgment was coming upon the old system, which
could not contain the fullness of what God desired to do. They killed
Stephen because of his witness, but they could not resist the wisdom
with which he spoke.

God did remember His mercy and truth to Israel: "He has
remembered His mercy and His faithfulness to the house of Israel;
all the ends of the earth have seen the salvation of our God" (Ps.
98:3). He saved the remnant before judging the nation. The result
would be that the nations would see the salvation of God. Salvation
could not come to the world until it first came to Israel.

A new song would be sung from the ends of the earth (Isa.
42:10). The new song is connected with the new creation. (See Psalm
40:3; 96:1; 98:1; 144:9; 149:1; and especially Revelation 5:9.) Nations
that did not know the God of Israel would know Him through salvation and would praise Him from the ends of the earth.

> Look to Me, and be saved, all you ends of the earth! For
> I am God, and there is no other.
>
> —ISAIAH 45:22

The nations that worshiped idols would come to the realization
that the God of Israel is the one true God. They would cast away
their idols and look to the Lord for salvation.

THE KINGDOM IN JERUSALEM

> When the Day of Pentecost had fully come, they were all with one accord in one place. And suddenly there came a sound from heaven, as of a rushing mighty wind, and it filled the whole house where they were sitting. Then there appeared to them divided tongues, as of fire, and one sat upon each of them. And they were all filled with the Holy Spirit and began to speak with other tongues, as the Spirit gave them utterance. And there were dwelling in Jerusalem Jews, devout men, from every nation under heaven. And when this sound occurred, the multitude came together, and were confused, because everyone heard them speak in his own language.
>
> —ACTS 2:1–6

Tongues are not a sign for them who believe—they are a sign for those who do not believe. Tongues got the attention of Jews from around the world. Undoubtedly many of them went back to their nations with the report of what they had seen on the Day of Pentecost. The kingdom, which began in Jerusalem, was to become a global phenomenon.

Tongues were also manifested in Samaria and in the house of Cornelius. When there was a significant breakthrough into new territory, tongues were evident. Tongues are a sign of the Holy Spirit and the presence of God. The expression of tongues is a sign of the presence of the kingdom of God.

Prayer, especially praying in tongues, is a vital aspect to our spiritual growth, to walking in the supernatural and being sensitive in the Spirit. The kingdom is advanced through the power of the Holy Spirit. Pentecost was necessary to release the church in the power of the Spirit. This was initiated through speaking in tongues.

The apostles immediately began to preach and minister in power. The result was an immediate increase in the number of disciples. The church grew quickly in Jerusalem in spite of hostility from many to the message of Christ. The church and the kingdom grew despite fierce persecution.

> Then those who gladly received his word were baptized; and that day about three thousand souls were added to them. And they continued steadfastly in the apostles' doctrine and fellowship, in the breaking of bread, and in prayers. Then fear came upon every soul, and many wonders and signs were done through the apostles.
>
> —ACTS 2:41–43

> Then the word of God spread, and the number of the disciples multiplied greatly in Jerusalem, and a great many of the priests were obedient to the faith.
>
> —ACTS 6:7

Many priests were obedient to the faith. This is a powerful testimony to the power of the kingdom. Many of the religious leaders, including the high priest, were enemies of the gospel. There were many, however, in the old-covenant temple system who embraced the kingdom.

God gave the apostles favor with the people (Acts 2:47). The King's favor is a powerful force in advancing the kingdom. Having favor with God and man is important to advance the kingdom. Favor is for the purpose of advancing the kingdom of God!

Local churches are an important part of advancing the kingdom. Many churches were formed after the Day of Pentecost: "So the churches were strengthened in the faith, and increased in number daily" (Acts 16:5). Church *planting* is also a major part of advancing the kingdom. C. Peter Wagner states:

The most concrete, lasting form of ministry in Acts is church planting. Preaching the gospel, healing the sick, casting out demons, suffering persecution, holding church councils and the multiple other activities of the apostles and other Christians that unfold before us have, as their goal, multiplying Christian churches throughout the known world. Related to his teaching of the kingdom, I would surmise that Jesus often repeated his purpose statement, "I will build my church" (Matt. 16:18).[4]

Churches need to be established in the faith. Churches established in the faith can increase daily. The local church is an agent of evangelism and the advancement of the kingdom. Church growth should be a normal part of the advancement of the kingdom.

> And through the hands of the apostles many signs and wonders were done among the people. And they were all with one accord in Solomon's Porch. Yet none of the rest dared join them, but the people esteemed them highly. And believers were increasingly added to the Lord, multitudes of both men and women.
>
> —Acts 5:12–14

Signs and wonders help advance the kingdom. These include miracles of healing and deliverance. There is no substitute for signs and wonders, and they were wrought by God in the early church. God will do His part if we preach the gospel. God is committed to advancing His kingdom in every generation.

THE KINGDOM COMES TO SAMARIA

> Then Philip went down to the city of Samaria and preached Christ to them. And the multitudes with one

> accord heeded the things spoken by Philip, hearing and
> seeing the miracles which he did. For unclean spirits,
> crying with a loud voice, came out of many who were
> possessed; and many who were paralyzed and lame
> were healed. And there was great joy in that city.
>
> —Acts 8:5–8

Acts records the gospel penetrating the city of Samaria. The Samaritans were a group who had split off from the Jewish people about six centuries earlier. They had intermarried with other peoples and were considered outsiders by most Jews. The Jews had no dealings with the Samaritans (John 4:9). The Jews looked on the Samaritans as second-class citizens. The Samaritans did not accept the full teaching of the Old Testament. They also worshiped in the wrong place—Mount Gerizim—not in Jerusalem. There were other major differences between the Jews in Christ's day and the Samaritans.

Luke records two incidents involving Samaritans that took place while Jesus was still on Earth. He tells of the good-heartedness of one Samaritan whom we commonly call the good Samaritan. The story is critical of a Jewish priest and a Levite but complimentary of a Samaritan (Luke 10:25–37). In another incident, Jesus healed ten lepers.

> And one of them, when he saw that he was healed,
> returned, and with a loud voice glorified God, and fell
> down on his face at His feet, giving Him thanks. And
> he was a Samaritan.
>
> —Luke 17:15–16

When Jesus spoke to the woman of Samaria, she believed and went and told the city. The whole city came out to meet Him (John 4:29–30). The implication is that the Samaritans were more open to the gospel than the legalistic, unbelieving Jews.

Deliverance from demons is a sign of the kingdom (Matt. 12:28).

Philip cast out demons in Samaria. The city had been bewitched by the sorcery of Simon. Wherever there is witchcraft and sorcery, there will be a great need for deliverance. When salvation comes, then comes deliverance. Salvation means deliverance.

Philip's preaching impacted the city of Samaria. People gave heed when they saw the miracles he did, and there was *great joy* in the city. Joy is another sign of the kingdom.

> Now when the apostles who were at Jerusalem heard that Samaria had received the word of God, they sent Peter and John to them, who, when they had come down, prayed for them that they might receive the Holy Spirit. For as yet He had fallen upon none of them. They had only been baptized in the name of the Lord Jesus. Then they laid hands on them, and they received the Holy Spirit.
>
> —ACTS 8:14–17

The preaching of the gospel with miracles following and people believing and being filled with the Holy Spirit is a pattern that we see in the advance of the kingdom. The apostles came from Jerusalem to lay hands on the new believers in Samaria, *confirming* them. This was proof that God honors the heart and not the nationality of a people. The Samaritans were loved by God, and salvation came to them in a powerful way.

THE KINGDOM COMES TO THE GENTILES

There are several verses from the Book of Acts concerning the Gentiles. These include:

- "…saying to Abraham, 'And in your seed all the families of the earth shall be blessed'" (Acts 3:25).

- "Go, for he is a chosen vessel of Mine to bear My name before Gentiles, kings..." (Acts 9:15).

- "In every nation whoever fears Him and works righteousness is accepted by Him" (Acts 10:35).

- "They glorified God, saying, 'Then God has also granted to the Gentiles repentance to life'" (Acts 11:18).

- "I have set you as a light to the Gentiles, that you should be for salvation to the ends of the earth" (Acts 13:47).

- "They reported all that God had done with them, and that He had opened the door of faith to the Gentiles" (Acts 14:27).

- "Therefore I want you to know that God's salvation has been sent to the Gentiles, and they will listen!" (Acts 28:28, NIV).

Peter preached in the house of Cornelius, and the Holy Spirit fell on Cornelius's household (Acts 10:44–48). Jews would not enter into a Gentile's house, and Peter was challenged by the disciples for doing so. He rehearsed to them what happened, and they realized that God had granted salvation to the Gentiles.

Receiving the Holy Spirit accompanies the advance of the kingdom. The coming in of the Gentiles was always the focus of the kingdom. The Jews were the first to come into the kingdom, and God's faithfulness and mercy to them opened the way for the nations to come under the rule of the Messiah.

Blindness began to come upon Israel as the kingdom advanced to the Gentiles. The coming in of the Gentiles was always the goal. This was the vision of the prophets—that through Israel salvation would go the ends of the earth. God used Israel to bring forth the Messiah, the Seed of Abraham, to be a blessing to all the families of the earth (Acts 13:47).

Paul was told to get out of Jerusalem and go to the Gentiles. This was all in the plan of God to advance the kingdom to the nations. He received this instruction while in a trance (Acts 16:9).

THE KINGDOM OF GOD IS CROSS-CULTURAL

Paul at Athens

> (All the Athenians and the foreigners who lived there spent their time doing nothing but talking about and listening to the latest ideas.) Paul then stood up in the meeting of the Areopagus and said: "Men of Athens! I see that in every way you are very religious. For as I walked around and looked carefully at your objects of worship, I even found an altar with this inscription: TO AN UNKNOWN GOD. Now what you worship as something unknown I am going to proclaim to you."
> —ACTS 17:21–23, NIV

The kingdom will bring salvation to different cultural groups. The apostles had to minister in cultures that were vastly different from the Hebrew culture in which they were raised. The Greek culture was much different from the Hebrew culture.

In his book *The Bible Exposition Commentary* Warren Wiersbe says this about Paul's gospel message to the Athenians (citing verse 16):

> Here Paul quoted from the poet Epimenides: "For in Him we live, and move, and have our being." Then he added a quotation from two poets, Aratus and Cleanthes, "For we are also His offspring."...This led to Paul's logical conclusion: God made us in His image, so it is foolish

for us to make gods in our own image! Greek religion was nothing but the manufacture and worship of gods who were patterned after men and who acted like men. Paul not only showed the folly of temples and the temple rituals, but also the folly of all idolatry.[5]

It is interesting that Paul quoted from Greek philosophers in presenting the gospel at Athens. Here Paul used a form of cultural exegesis to show the people the folly in their worship of idols and the importance of worshiping the only God, who is the God-Man Jesus Christ. Paul took the time to understand them enough to quote back to them their own philosophers to use those portions of culture to point to Jesus.

In his blog, youth pastor Marv Nelson suggests the following:

We should look at preaching the gospel in such a way as Paul did: it is for all people, and we must become all things to all people for the sake of saving some (1 Cor. 9:22). This means that if we desire to tell a certain people group the truths laid out in the Scripture, we must study that culture. We must observe them and become wise people as to how they live. We must figure out how to best communicate the truth to them to ensure that they receive it. If we fail to study people of different cultures and fail to see how best to communicate to them the truth of the gospel, we will have done wrong. We, like Paul, need to have a spiritual provocation to action; then we need to start learning as much as we can about those we expect to teach.[6]

A different language means a different culture, different music, and different habits. The ability of the kingdom to cross cultural barriers is evident in the Book of Acts. The gospel has relevance in any culture. It is *good news* to everyone. There are people in every culture who desire the *peace* that comes with the kingdom of God.

> After these things I looked, and behold, a great multitude which no one could number, of all nations, tribes, peoples, and tongues, standing before the throne and before the Lamb, clothed with white robes, with palm branches in their hands, and crying out with a loud voice, saying, "Salvation belongs to our God who sits on the throne, and to the Lamb!"
>
> —REVELATION 7:9–10

All nations, kindreds, people, and tongues stand on Mount Zion. They all attribute salvation to the King and to the Lamb. The kingdom cannot be limited to a certain culture. This is because the kingdom message goes beyond the culture and touches the spirit.

The culture of the kingdom

There is also a culture of the kingdom of God. The culture of the kingdom transcends all human cultures. New believers must be taught the characteristics and culture of the kingdom. The culture of the kingdom includes love, humility, service, integrity, forgiveness, work, giving, worship, prayer, respect, honor, and so forth.

The culture of the kingdom will challenge the unrighteousness that is resident in many cultures. It will challenge us in areas of our culture where sin is acceptable.

The kingdom of God went into many pagan cultures. These cultures were filled with idolatry and superstition. Sexual immorality was common in these cultures. The Western culture of today is also filled with immorality, because it has roots in paganism.

Camille Paglia writes, "Western culture is a very complex combination of two traditions—the Judeo-Christian and the Greco-Roman. The overarching argument of all of my work is that paganism was never in fact defeated by Christianity but instead went underground to resurface at three key moments: the Renaissance, Romanticism, and twentieth-century popular culture, whose sex and violence I interpret as pagan phenomena."[7]

Those who receive the gospel will dissociate themselves from sexual immorality. Paul admonished the church at Ephesus, "But fornication and all uncleanness or covetousness, let it not even be named among you, as is fitting for saints" (Eph. 5:3). Early church leaders stressed that abstaining from fornication is God's will for believers: "For this is the will of God, your sanctification: that you should abstain from sexual immorality" (1 Thess. 4:3).

A decree was issued by the Jerusalem Council that the Gentiles were to abstain from fornication.

> But concerning the Gentiles who believe, we have written and decided that they should observe no such thing, except that they should keep themselves from things offered to idols, from blood, from things strangled, and from sexual immorality.
>
> —ACTS 21:25

Fornication is the Greek word *porneia*, which has a broad-based meaning, including "illicit sexual intercourse, adultery, homosexuality, lesbianism, intercourse with animals, etc.; sexual intercourse with close relatives (Lev. 18); sexual intercourse with a divorced man or woman; and the worship of idols of the defilement of idolatry, as incurred by eating the sacrifices offered to idols."[8]

Speaking of the Greek culture Paul addressed, Doyle Lynch writes:

> The dominant culture in the establishment of the kingdom was the Greek culture. The world in which Paul lived was a Greek (Hellenized) world, thanks to

Alexander the Great, who made it his mission to make the world Greek. By his death in 323 B.C., much of the known world was ruled by Greece. Greek culture was forced upon the world. Even when Rome became the ruler of the world just before the time of Christ, it adopted much of Greek culture. The Greeks were learned and skilled in the arts. They referred to the non-Greek as a *Barbarian*. They gave culture a new meaning.

They were also a morally corrupt people. Immorality and promiscuity were rampant and considered normal. Divorce was common. Homosexuality was viewed as normal by many Greeks. Those familiar with Greek mythology will know that the Greek gods were no better than the Greeks themselves. Paul was not exaggerating when he said many Christians had formerly walked in immorality, impurity, passion, evil desire, greed and idolatry (Colossians 3:5–6). It is not amazing that many Jewish Christians did not warmly accept Greeks who were newly converted to Christianity.[9]

The advance of the kingdom in the Greek world is a testimony to the power of the kingdom.

All these things the pagans seek. Your heavenly Father knows that you need them all. But seek first the kingdom (of God) and his righteousness, and all these things will be given you besides.
—MATTHEW 6:32–34, NAB

God created a holy people in the midst of idolatry and perversion. The same is true today. The gospel has the power to overcome the immorality of Western culture today.

Jesus contrasts those in the kingdom with pagans. A *pagan* is defined as "an adherent of a polytheistic religion in antiquity, especially when viewed in contrast to an adherent of a monotheistic religion." Paul cautioned the Corinthian church about the need to avoid fellowship with pagans who might be under the influence of a demonic being because of their sacrifices.

> No, I am suggesting that what the pagans sacrifice they offer [in effect] to demons (to evil spiritual powers) and not to God [at all]. I do not want you to fellowship and be partners with diabolical spirits [by eating at their feasts].
>
> —1 CORINTHIANS 10:20, AMP

Pagans worship demons (idols). Their worship involved temple prostitutes (sodomites). It was into this pagan world that the kingdom was established.

The Greeks had many gods, including Aphrodite, the goddess of love, who was the most beautiful among the Olympian goddesses. An aristocratic woman named Sappho, who lived on the island *Lesbos* in the Aegean Sea near Greece, worshiped Aphrodite and frequently mentioned the goddess in her poetry, admiring her and asking for her help in her relationships with women. It because of Sappho and the name of the island on which she lived that we get the modern word *lesbian*.

Sexual immorality and perversion are pagan and are rooted in idolatry. (See Romans 1.) The Gentiles suppressed the truth of God and spiraled into idolatry and sexual immorality.

The culture of the kingdom is one of holiness and sexual purity. Those who submit to Christ and the kingdom will present their bodies as living sacrifices, holy and acceptable to God.

The people to whom Jesus was speaking were covering up their lusts and sexual sin with divorce, and Jesus warned His followers about this.

> But I say to you that whoever divorces his wife for
> any reason except sexual immorality causes her to
> commit adultery; and whoever marries a woman who
> is divorced commits adultery.
>
> —MATTHEW 5:32

The Pharisees were covetous, greedy, and lustful. They were adulterers who appeared to be righteous outwardly but inwardly were unrighteous. By contrast, sexual purity and fidelity are marks of the kingdom.

In the kingdom men are admonished to love their wives as Christ loved the church. Men are to respect their wives as joint heirs of the grace of God. This is the opposite of the hardness of heart that many men had toward their wives. (See Matthew 19.)

At the time of the early church, all that was required for divorce was a certificate written by a dissatisfied husband. We must recall that at Christ's time a divorced woman had very little left to her in life—just difficulty supporting herself and a lack of social status. Divorce had become a legal process with no mercy and compassion shown to the women who were put away. We will take at closer look at the role of women in the kingdom in the following chapter.

CHAPTER 10

WOMEN AND THE KINGDOM

THERE ARE MANY examples in the Scriptures of women operating in the kingdom of God. In Christ there is neither male nor female (Gal. 2:28). Women have equal access to the blessings of the kingdom. Women are not second-class citizens in the kingdom. Jesus elevated women above the culture of their day. Jesus elevated women above the status given them by society.

> [Many] Jews had a very dim view of women. Jewish women were not allowed to receive an education. Hence, they were largely uneducated. Their only training was in how to raise children and keep house.
> Women were also largely excluded from worshiping God. In Herod's temple, there was a special court that stood on the very outside. It was called the Court of the Gentiles. The Gentiles could go into that court, but

they were limited to that area alone. Five steps above the Gentiles court was the women's court. The women were limited to that one area. Fifteen steps above that was the Jewish men's court. Thus men were given far more privileges to worship God than were women.

A woman had no voice in her marriage. Her father decided whom she would marry, when she would marry, and why she would marry. A woman couldn't divorce her husband under any condition. Only a man could initiate a divorce.

Jewish women were to be seen as little as possible in public. In fact, young men were warned about talking to women in public, so much so that it was a shame in ancient Israel for a man to talk to a woman in public. Consequently, most women stayed out of the streets.

Women were regarded as inferior to men. They were regarded as property, just like cattle and slaves. Jewish males prayed a daily prayer of thanksgiving. This prayer shows how poorly the Jews looked upon women. It goes like this:

- Praise be to God. He has not created me a Gentile.

- Praise be to God. He has not created me a woman.

- Praise be to God. He has not created me an ignorant man.

This was man's view of a woman in first-century Israel. It was not much better in other cultures. In fact, ever since the Fall of humanity, women have been regarded as second-class citizens—inferior to men. But something happened that changed all that.

Jesus came![1]

The Pharisees had no compassion for women. They were greedy and took advantage of widows. Jesus defended widows against the greed of these hypocritical leaders. Jesus loves women and has compassion on them.

Jesus came to liberate the daughters of Abraham. Jesus healed a woman with a spirit of infirmity and rebuked the Pharisees for their lack of compassion. They had more compassion for their animals than for this woman. The Pharisees were ashamed, but the people rejoiced.

> Now He was teaching in one of the synagogues on the Sabbath. And behold, there was a woman who had a spirit of infirmity eighteen years, and was bent over and could in no way raise herself up. But when Jesus saw her, He called her to Him and said to her, "Woman, you are loosed from your infirmity." And He laid His hands on her, and immediately she was made straight, and glorified God. But the ruler of the synagogue answered with indignation, because Jesus had healed on the Sabbath; and he said to the crowd, "There are six days on which men ought to work; therefore come and be healed on them, and not on the Sabbath day." The Lord then answered him and said, "Hypocrite! Does not each one of you on the Sabbath loose his ox or donkey from the stall, and lead it away to water it? So ought not this woman, being a daughter of Abraham, whom Satan has bound—think of it—for eighteen years, be loosed from this bond on the Sabbath?" And when He said these things, all His adversaries were put to shame; and all the multitude rejoiced for all the glorious things that were done by Him.
>
> —LUKE 13:10–17

The kingdom puts honor on widows: "Honor widows who are really widows" (1 Tim. 5:3). James tells the believers the definition of pure and undefiled religion in James 1:27:

> Pure and undefiled religion before God and the Father
> is this: to visit orphans and widows in their trouble,
> and to keep oneself unspotted from the world.

Many cultures have a very low view of women. This was certainly true in early rabbinic expositions of Jewish law. One example states:

> A man should ever avoid women; thus he should never
> make any gestures at them, either with his hands or his
> feet, nor wink at them, nor jest with them…A man
> must not greet a woman under any circumstances, and
> he is forbidden to send his regards to her even through
> her husband.[2]

This will be challenged and corrected when the kingdom is preached and received. This is why we must preach the kingdom. The kingdom liberates women from the constraints of culture.

Although these *laws* were not found in the Bible, they were often generally understood *traditions of men* at the time of Christ.

JESUS AND WOMEN

Jesus broke these traditions of men by interacting with women. He conversed with a Samaritan woman in Samaria (John 4). He allowed a woman to anoint Him for burial (Mark 14:3–9; Matt. 26:6–13). He forgave a woman taken in adultery (John 8:2–11). Mary and Martha were good friends with Jesus (Luke 10:38–42).

Jesus regularly ministered to women, often healing them. The woman with the issue of blood had suffered with an incurable flow of blood for twelve long years before Jesus healed her (Mark 5:25–34;

see also Luke 8:43–48; Matt. 9:20–22). For all that time she had been ritually unclean, as indicated in the Law.

In Luke 8 we have an account of His interaction with some women to whom He had already ministered:

> Now it came to pass, afterward, that He went through every city and village, preaching and bringing the glad tidings of the kingdom of God. And the twelve were with Him, and certain women who had been healed of evil spirits and infirmities—Mary called Magdalene, out of whom had come seven demons, and Joanna the wife of Chuza, Herod's steward, and Susanna, and many others who provided for Him from their substance.
>
> —Luke 8:1–3

These women were healed of evil spirits and infirmities, and they followed Christ, ministering to Him from their substance. Our Lord's practice of being supported by women affirmed the importance of women in the proclamation of the gospel and the practical partnership attained by underwriting the preaching of the gospel.

There were many women who followed Jesus and ministered to Him. It was a woman who brought the message of Christ's resurrection to the disciples.

> Then they returned from the tomb and told all these things to the eleven and to all the rest. It was Mary Magdalene, Joanna, Mary the mother of James, and the other women with them, who told these things to the apostles. And their words seemed to them like idle tales, and they did not believe them.
>
> —Luke 24:9–11

Perhaps the reason the apostles did not believe the women was because there was such a prevalent climate in Israel at that time that disdained women and refused to recognize their position in the kingdom.

Women were also involved in the prayer in the Upper Room before Pentecost.

> These all continued with one accord in prayer and sup-plication, with the women and Mary the mother of Jesus, and with His brothers.
>
> —ACTS 1:14

WOMEN IN THE NEW TESTAMENT CHURCH

Philip had four daughters who prophesied (Acts 21:9). When teaching about the gifts of the Spirit, Paul admonishes that we are all encour-aged to prophesy (1 Cor. 14:5). Prophecy is one of the recognizable characteristics of life in the kingdom of God. When Peter preached his landmark sermon on the Day of Pentecost, he included Joel's pro-phetic words in the Old Testament:

> And it shall come to pass in the last days, says God,
> That I will pour out of My Spirit on all flesh;
> Your sons and your daughters shall prophesy,
> Your young men shall see visions,
> Your old men shall dream dreams.
>
> —ACTS 2:17

He was carefully indicating to the people that the prophecies had been fulfilled with the coming of Christ and that men *and* women would share equally in the blessings and benefits of kingdom living.

In spite of the coming of Christ, women were still treated as second-class citizens by many Jews. Before his dramatic entrance into the kingdom, Saul, the persecutor of the church, put women as well as men in prison for their faith (Acts 8:3). After his conversion we see a dramatic change in this former persecutor of women. Many women labored with Paul in the gospel. In Philippians Paul writes, "And I urge you also, true companion, help these women who labored with me in the gospel, with Clement also, and the rest of my fellow workers, whose names are in the Book of Life" (Phil. 4:3).

A KINGDOM PERSPECTIVE ON WOMEN

Wherever the kingdom advances, women are healed and restored in Christ. Women become active participants in ministry, along with men, in promoting the kingdom of God. Women are key and instrumental for the growth of the kingdom.

One sex is not to be regarded as the special favorite of heaven and the other to be excluded. Christianity thus elevates the female sex to an equality with the male on the most important of all interests. In this way it has made most important changes in the world wherever it has prevailed.

In his reference *Barnes' Notes on the New Testament,* Albert Barnes observes:

> Everywhere, but in connection with the Christian religion, woman has been degraded. She has been kept in ignorance. She has been treated as an inferior in all respects. She has been doomed to unpitied drudgery, and ignorance, and toil. So she was among the ancient Greeks and Romans; so she is in China, and India, and in the islands of the sea; so she is regarded in the Koran, and in all Muslim countries. It is Christianity alone which has elevated her; and nowhere on earth does man regard the mother of his children as an intelligent companion and friend, except where the influence of the Christian religion has been felt. At the

communion table, at the foot of the cross, and in the hopes of heaven, she is on a level with man; and this fact diffuses a mild, and purifying, and elevating influence over all the relations of life. Woman has been raised from deep degradation by the influence of Christianity; and, let me add, she has everywhere acknowledged the debt of gratitude, and devoted herself, as under a deep sense of obligation, to lessening the burdens of humanity, and to the work of elevating the degraded, instructing the ignorant, and comforting the afflicted, all over the world. Never has a debt been better repaid, or the advantages of elevating one portion of the race been more apparent.[3]

This is why women respond so well to the preaching and demonstration of the gospel of the kingdom. The kingdom *liberates* women from oppression. In the kingdom women are respected and honored.

Some have used Paul's words concerning women being silent in the church to imply that Paul had a dislike and low opinion of women (1 Cor. 14:34). It is important to note the historical context of Paul's admonition to the Corinthians.

In F. F. Bruce's *The New Century Bible Commentary, 1 and 2 Corinthians*, Bruce notes that Paul had already recognized a woman's right to pray and prophesy in the church prior to his letter to the Corinthians. Therefore the imposition of silence and forbidding women to speak is only in the context of interrupting the proceedings by asking questions of their husbands. Asking questions should be done at home. Bruce carefully notes that Paul's admonitions in 1 Corinthians 14:34–35 related to women speaking in church are limited in application and refer only to the interrupting of proceedings.[4]

There are no *male* or *female* gifts. Further proof that Paul did not limit women's participation in the church services of the churches is found in this same letter:

And God has appointed these in the church: first apostles, second prophets, third teachers, after that miracles, then gifts of healings, helps, administrations, varieties of tongues. Are all apostles? Are all prophets? Are all teachers? Are all workers of miracles? Do all have gifts of healings? Do all speak with tongues? Do all interpret? But earnestly desire the best gifts.

—1 CORINTHIANS 12:28–31

Dianne D. McDonnell notes:

There is not a single scripture that lists some of these gifts as "male gifts" and some of these as "female gifts." Paul argues that each person receives a gift and advises all to "desire the best gifts"! Would he say that if any of the top five gifts were off-limits to women?[5]

Likewise, Mimi Haddad writes:

Though Paul asks women to remain silent when their voices contributed to disorderly worship, this injunction does not limit their voices in all places at all times. Remember, women were prominent as prophets in both the Old Testament (Numbers 12:1-16, Judges 4:4-5, 5:7, 2 Kings 22:14) and the New Testament. Women prophets were active at Pentecost (Acts 2:17), Phillip had four prophesying daughters (Acts 21:9), and there were women prophets mentioned in Paul's letter to the church in Corinth (1 Corinthians 11:5). Paul exhorts all Christians in Corinth to seek the gift of prophecy. The gift of prophecy was given to men as well as women. Women and men may speak in churches today as long as their voices do not distract those who need to hear the gospel![6]

The kingdom is INCLUSIVE and is open to all races and both genders. This breaks down the strongholds of racism and sexism. This is why the gospel is good news. The gospel is liberating and causes rejoicing to those that hear. The gospel brings salvation to all who hear and believe.

Women play an important part in advancing the kingdom. They can be anointed to pray, preach, prophesy, and do the works of Christ. Great advancement occurs whenever women are released. Societies are changed and advance when women take their rightful place in the kingdom.

There is much work to be done in many nations, but the gospel is the power that brings change. There is a great blessing that occurs anywhere people are liberated and released to live their lives with purpose and destiny. We can be assured that as the kingdom increases, women will be set free to receive and be a blessing.

CHAPTER 11

THE TOOLS OF ADVANCEMENT

A S NEW MEMBERS of the kingdom of God, God makes available to us several important tools that will help us to understand better the King and His kingdom. In this chapter we are going to take a close look at some of these tools.

VISIONS ADVANCE THE KINGDOM

Visions and trances were a part of advancing the kingdom in the early days of the birth of the church. In the Book of Acts, we read that Paul received a message from God through a trance that told him that God was going to send him to the Gentiles.

> Now it happened, when I returned to Jerusalem and was praying in the temple, that I was in a trance and saw Him saying to me, "Make haste and get out of

Jerusalem quickly, for they will not receive your testimony concerning Me." So I said, "Lord, they know that in every synagogue I imprisoned and beat those who believe on You. And when the blood of Your martyr Stephen was shed, I also was standing by consenting to his death, and guarding the clothes of those who were killing him." Then He said to me, "Depart, for I will send you far from here to the Gentiles."

—ACTS 22:17–21

Peter also fell into a trance and had a vision, instructing him to go to the house of Cornelius. His vision of eating unclean animals was to prepare him to minister to the Gentiles, whom Israel considered unclean.

Then he became very hungry and wanted to eat; but while they made ready, he fell into a trance and saw heaven opened and an object like a great sheet bound at the four corners, descending to him and let down to the earth. In it were all kinds of four-footed animals of the earth, wild beasts, creeping things, and birds of the air. And a voice came to him, "Rise, Peter; kill and eat." But Peter said, "Not so, Lord! For I have never eaten anything common or unclean." And a voice spoke to him again the second time, "What God has cleansed you must not call common."

—ACTS 10:10–15

Once he began his ministry to Gentiles, Paul had other visions that were tools God was using to direct his work in specific directions. He heard the call to Macedonia in a vision. He went to Macedonia and preached the gospel.

> And a vision appeared to Paul in the night. A man of
> Macedonia stood and pleaded with him, saying, "Come
> over to Macedonia and help us."
>
> —ACTS 16:9

Trances and visions are a part of advancing the kingdom. These supernatural encounters help us to break through into new territories and regions.

Paul's calling came through a vision of the risen Lord. Paul was not disobedient to the heavenly vision. We must have vision to advance the kingdom. We must have God's vision for the territories to which we are sent. Paul began experiencing visions from God as early as the moment of his conversion on a Damascus road. As he stood before King Agrippa making a defense against all the false accusations of the Jews, he told the king of his early life spent in Jerusalem surrounded by Jews who knew him. They knew he was faithful to the laws and traditions of the strictest sect of Jews and that he lived his life as a Pharisee. He told of his persecution to the Jews who believed in Jesus, even casting his vote against them to condemn them to death.

Then he explained to King Agrippa that he was now being judged by the Jews because of the eternal hope he had found through the redemption that was his because of the death and resurrection of Jesus Christ, whom the Jews would not accept. He tells of his moment of conversion:

> And when we all had fallen to the ground, I heard a
> voice speaking to me and saying in the Hebrew lan-
> guage, "Saul, Saul, why are you persecuting Me? It is
> hard for you to kick against the goads." So I said, "Who
> are You, Lord?" And He said, "I am Jesus, whom you
> are persecuting. But rise and stand on your feet; for I
> have appeared to you for this purpose, to make you a

> minister and a witness both of the things which you have seen and of the things which I will yet reveal to you. I will deliver you from the Jewish people, as well as from the Gentiles, to whom I now send you, to open their eyes, in order to turn them from darkness to light, and from the power of Satan to God, that they may receive forgiveness of sins and an inheritance among those who are sanctified by faith in Me."
>
> —ACTS 26:14–18

After he told the king of his conversion, he said, "Therefore, King Agrippa, I was not disobedient to the heavenly vision, but declared first to those in Damascus and in Jerusalem, and throughout all the region of Judea, and then to the Gentiles, that they should repent, turn to God, and do works befitting repentance" (Acts 26:19–20).

This heavenly vision was the catalyst to see the kingdom advance from Damascus, Jerusalem, Judea, and to the Gentiles.

We again see deliverance from demons through the ministry of Paul at Ephesus. The city was a center of occult activity, and God wrought special miracles by Paul, with the result being sickness and demons leaving people through handkerchiefs and aprons.

> Now God worked unusual miracles by the hands of Paul, so that even handkerchiefs or aprons were brought from his body to the sick, and the diseases left them and the evil spirits went out of them.
>
> —ACTS 19:11–12

DELIVERANCE—AN IMPORTANT ASPECT OF THE KINGDOM

The kingdom of God was challenging and overpowering the rule of Satan over the nations. Deliverance is common when there is idolatry, occultism, witchcraft, and sorcery present in the lives of people. When people come under the rule of God, the power of Satan is broken.

The miraculous is an important aspect of the kingdom of God. Deliverance from demons is a miracle ministry. Jesus began with the message of the kingdom. He preached this message throughout Galilee and cast out devils (Mark 1:39).

Jesus cast out *many devils*. This was an integral part of His ministry. Jesus demonstrated the authority of the kingdom over the powers of darkness.

> Then He healed many who were sick with various dis-
> eases, and cast out many demons; and He did not allow
> the demons to speak, because they knew Him.
> —MARK 1:34

The disciples also cast out many devils. They also preached the kingdom of God. They anointed many with oil and healed them. "And they cast out many demons, and anointed with oil many who were sick, and healed them" (Mark 6:13). Those in bondage to sickness and demons were set free. This was the good news of the kingdom of God.

Too often the church has tried to advance the kingdom without the supernatural. Many have shied away from deliverance because of the fear and ignorance often encountered in this area. We must remember that this is the ministry of Christ. Christ had compassion on the sick and demonized, and so should we. The ministry of Christ continues through His church. This is a sign that should follow believers (Mark 16:17).

The Kingdom Advanced Through Prayer

I call prayer the engine of the kingdom. The disciples were told to pray, "Thy kingdom come" (Matt. 6:10, KJV). This means that the kingdom could not come or advance apart from prayer. Even the Son is to ask the Father, "Ask of me, and I will make the nations your inheritance, the ends of the earth your possession" (Ps. 2:8, NIV).

There were people praying before the arrival of the kingdom, like Anna, a prophetess.

> There was also a prophetess, Anna, the daughter of Phanuel, of the tribe of Asher. She was very old; she had lived with her husband seven years after her marriage, and then was a widow until she was eighty-four. She never left the temple but worshiped night and day, fasting and praying. Coming up to them at that very moment, she gave thanks to God and spoke about the child to all who were looking forward to the redemption of Jerusalem.
>
> —Luke 2:36–38, NIV

She did not depart from the temple but served God with fasting and prayer night and day. There were undoubtedly others praying that are not recorded in Scripture. These prayers and intercessions were used by God to help inaugurate the kingdom.

Prayer was a very necessary thing for Jesus as He assumed His ministry on Earth. He prayed for nights as He was preaching the kingdom: "Very early in the morning, while it was still dark, Jesus got up, left the house and went off to a solitary place, where he prayed" (Mark 1:35, NIV). He needed to be in constant, direct communication with His Father in heaven. Jesus prayed all night before choosing the Twelve.

> One of those days Jesus went out to a mountainside
> to pray, and spent the night praying to God. When
> morning came, he called his disciples to him and chose
> twelve of them, whom he also designated apostles.
>
> —LUKE 6:12–13, NIV

Prayer was a part of His ministry and an important part of advancing the kingdom.

Prayer was the key to the outpouring of the Holy Spirit. After the ascension of Jesus to heaven, the apostles returned immediately to Jerusalem, where they gathered in the Upper Room. Other believers soon joined them, and they continued, "constantly in prayer" (Acts 1:14, NIV). On the Day of Pentecost, 120 believers were already assembled in the Upper Room, praying.

> When the day of Pentecost came, they were all together in
> one place. Suddenly a sound like the blowing of a violent
> wind came from heaven and filled the whole house where
> they were sitting. They saw what seemed to be tongues
> of fire that separated and came to rest on each of them.
> All of them were filled with the Holy Spirit and began to
> speak in other tongues as the Spirit enabled them.
>
> —ACTS 2:1–4, NIV

There have been outpourings of the Spirit in history because of prayer. The church continued in prayer after Pentecost. The church was a prayer *engine* for the advancement of the kingdom.

> They devoted themselves to the apostles' teaching and
> to the fellowship, to the breaking of bread and to prayer.
>
> —ACTS 2:42, NIV

The apostles gave themselves continually to prayer.

> Brothers, choose seven men from among you who are
> known to be full of the Spirit and wisdom. We will
> turn this responsibility [care of widows] over to them
> and will give our attention to prayer and the ministry
> of the word.
>
> —ACTS 6:3–4, NIV

Their diligence to prayer and the Word was a key to their success in ministry. Apostolic ministry is a ministry of prayer and the Word.

A devout and God-fearing centurion in Caesarea received a vision, and an angel of God came to him and told him, "Your prayers and gifts to the poor have come up as a memorial offering before God" (Acts 10:4). The angel instructed him to send servants to Joppa, where they would find Peter, who they were to bring back to Caesarea. As a result of his faithfulness in prayer, Cornelius was a key to opening the door for the kingdom to come to the Gentiles. God responded to Cornelius's prayer and giving. Cornelius told Peter:

> Four days ago I was in my house praying at this hour,
> at three in the afternoon. Suddenly a man in shining
> clothes stood before me and said, "Cornelius, God has
> heard your prayer and remembered your gifts to the
> poor. Send to Joppa for Simon who is called Peter. He is
> a guest in the home of Simon the tanner, who lives by
> the sea." So I sent for you immediately, and it was good
> of you to come. Now we are all here in the presence of
> God to listen to everything the Lord has commanded
> you to tell us.
>
> —ACTS 10:30–33, NIV

Upon hearing Cornelius's words, Peter began to tell him of Jesus's death and resurrection and that Jesus had instructed His disciples to "preach to the people and to testify that he is the one whom

God appointed as judge of the living and the dead" (Acts 10:42, NIV). The Word tells us:

> While Peter was still speaking these words, the Holy Spirit came on all who heard the message. The circumcised believers who had come with Peter were astonished that the gift of the Holy Spirit had been poured out even on the Gentiles. For they heard them speaking in tongues and praising God.
>
> —ACTS 10:44–46, NIV

When the church began to face persecution, they prayed with powerful results. They prayed for boldness and for the Lord to stretch forth His hand with healing, signs, and wonders.

PRAYER COMBINED WITH FASTING

Prayer, coupled with fasting, releases tremendous power for breakthrough. Fasting helps overcome stubborn obstacles and barriers to kingdom advancement (2 Cor. 11:27). The New King James Version of the Bible indicates that Cornelius was praying *and* fasting when he received the visitation from an angel that initiated the kingdom coming to the Gentiles: "So Cornelius said, 'Four days ago I was fasting until this hour; and at the ninth hour I prayed in my house, and behold, a man stood before me in bright clothing'" (Acts 10:30). Fasting causes humility, which gets the attention of God. God gives grace to the humble.

The prophets and teachers of the church at Antioch ministered to the Lord and fasted. They received instruction from the Holy Spirit to separate Barnabas and Paul for apostolic ministry. The apostles were then sent forth by the church after fasting.

> Now in the church that was at Antioch there were certain prophets and teachers: Barnabas, Simeon who was

called Niger, Lucius of Cyrene, Manaen who had been
brought up with Herod the tetrarch, and Saul. As they
ministered to the Lord and fasted, the Holy Spirit said,
"Now separate to Me Barnabas and Saul for the work
to which I have called them." Then, having fasted and
prayed, and laid hands on them, they sent them away.

—ACTS 13:1–3

Paul and Barnabas were used by God to bring the kingdom to
the Gentiles.

The Antioch church became an apostolic sending center that
affected the nations. This church released two of their best leaders
and sent them at the direction of the Holy Spirit. Through this we
can see that the Holy Spirit is active in advancing the kingdom.

The kingdom is spiritual, and prayer and fasting are spiritual
acts. Spiritual people are used by God to advance His kingdom.
People motivated by the Holy Spirit to pray and fast are those who
are the vessels of kingdom advancement.

THE ROLE OF PERSECUTION IN ADVANCING THE KINGDOM

Another important message in the Book of Acts is that the kingdom
advances in spite of persecution. The early church was persecuted
and considered to be a heretical sect.

At that time a great persecution arose against the
church which was at Jerusalem; and they were all scattered throughout the regions of Judea and Samaria,
except the apostles.

—ACTS 8:1

Persecution is always intended to stop momentum. Because
of the persecution of believers that continued after the stoning of

Stephen, the church at Jerusalem was scattered throughout all of Judea.

The persecution caused the disciples to scatter and preach the Word to the Jews only. God was reaching out to the lost sheep of Israel outside of Jerusalem. God would eventually use Philip and Paul to go outside of Israel to the Gentiles.

Some of the major persecution came from the Jews. They were fierce persecutors of Paul.

> But the Jews stirred up the devout and prominent women and the chief men of the city, raised up persecution against Paul and Barnabas, and expelled them from their region.
>
> —ACTS 13:50

Many felt Paul was an apostate because of his ministry and fellowship with the Gentiles. Paul was a believing Pharisee who understood the grace of God and salvation. He was not an apostate but a faithful Jew who understood the promises of God to Israel and the world. Paul believed all things that were written in the Law and Prophets (Acts 24:14).

Paul only preached the hope of Israel. The problem was that many of the Jews did not understand their own Scriptures. They could not see the mystery of the kingdom.

The wisdom of Gamaliel

Gamaliel was a Pharisee and a teacher of the Law who was honored by all of the people. When the high priest and all his associates became jealous of the ministry of the apostles and arrested them and put them in jail, an angel of the Lord opened the doors of the jail and brought them out (Acts 5:23). The apostles went straight to the temple and again began preaching. They were again apprehended and brought before the Sanhedrin to be questioned. The apostles' answer to their questioning infuriated the high priest, and the Sanhedrin wanted to put them to death.

But Gamaliel stood up and addressed the Sanhedrin:

> Therefore, in the present case I advise you: Leave these men alone! Let them go! For if their purpose or activity is of human origin, it will fail. But if it is from God, you will not be able to stop these men; you will only find yourselves fighting against God.
>
> —ACTS 5:38–39, NIV

Many of that generation refused to hear the wisdom of Gamaliel. Gamaliel understood that you cannot fight against the purpose of God. The kingdom is God's purpose, and you cannot fight against it. The kingdom always prevails. The kingdom always advances from generation to generation.

God used persecution to get the message outside of Jerusalem to Samaria and to the uttermost part of the earth. Persecution, meant for evil, is turned to good by the wisdom of God. There is no wisdom or counsel against the Lord. The wisdom of the kingdom always defeats the wisdom of hell.

Imprisonment, beatings, threats, and death could not stop the kingdom from advancing. Jesus had warned the disciples what they would experience when He sent them to preach the kingdom.

> Be on your guard against men; they will hand you over to the local councils and flog you in their synagogues. On my account you will be brought before governors and kings as witnesses to them and to the Gentiles.
>
> —MATTHEW 10:17–18, NIV

Much of the opposition came from the established religious system of that day. The message of the kingdom exposed the rebellion and hypocrisy of that system. The kingdom was coming to remove the old covenant system in judgment. The establishment of the new covenant meant the vanishing away of the old covenant. The old often fights the new at own its peril and demise.

FAITH AND THE KINGDOM

Faith is the key governing principle that underscores successful operation in the kingdom of God on Earth. It is obvious that many did not enter the kingdom because of unbelief. Jesus actually marveled at the unbelief of many in Israel.

> Jesus left there and went to his hometown, accompanied by his disciples. When the Sabbath came, he began to teach in the synagogue, and many who heard him were amazed. "Where did this man get these things?" they asked. "What's this wisdom that has been given him, that he even does miracles? Isn't this the carpenter? Isn't this Mary's son and the brother of James, Joseph, Judas and Simon? Aren't his sisters here with us?" And they took offense at him. Jesus said to them, "Only in his hometown, among his relatives and in his own house is a prophet without honor." He could not do any miracles there, except lay his hands on a few sick people and heal them. And he was amazed at their lack of faith.
>
> —MARK 6:1–6, NIV

The kingdom will not operate where there is no faith. Jesus could not find great faith in Israel. Faith and power are the keys to operating in the miraculous and demonstrating the kingdom. Because Stephen was full of faith and power, he was able to perform great wonders and signs among the people (Acts 6:8).

Jesus found more faith with Gentiles than He did with Israel.

The Roman centurion exhibited great faith. The centurion understood authority and had no problem believing that Jesus could speak the word and his servant would be healed.

> When Jesus heard this, he was amazed at him, and turning to the crowd following him, he said, "I tell you, I have not found such great faith even in Israel."
>
> —LUKE 7:9, NIV

The centurion was a Gentile, yet he had more faith than those of Israel. This was a sign that the Gentiles would believe, even while Israel was in unbelief.

Publicans and harlots would enter the kingdom before the Pharisees because they believed. Jesus told the chief priests and elders in the temple, "I tell you the truth, the tax collectors and the prostitutes are entering the kingdom of God ahead of you. For John came to you to show you the way of righteousness, and you did not believe him, but the tax collectors and the prostitutes did. And even after you saw this, you did not repent and believe him" (Matt. 21:31–32, NIV). Unbelief would keep many out of the kingdom.

Those who repented and believed received the kingdom.

One of the strongest words Jesus spoke to unbelieving Israel is found in Matthew chapter 8.

> When Jesus heard this, he was amazed and said to those following him, "Truly I tell you, I have not found anyone in Israel with such great faith. I say to you that many will come from the east and the west, and will take their places at the feast with Abraham, Isaac and Jacob in the kingdom of heaven. But the subjects of the kingdom will be thrown outside, into the darkness, where there will be weeping and gnashing of teeth."
>
> —MATTHEW 8:10–12, NIV

The children of the kingdom (the Jews) would be shut out, while the Gentiles would enter. The key is faith. God honors faith. God only respects faith.

It takes faith to heal the sick, cast out devils, and prophesy. It takes faith to operate in the power of the kingdom. Faith removes mountains. It takes faith to enter the kingdom and live in the kingdom.

Barnabas was a good man, full of faith, and because he was, many people were added to the Lord (Acts 11:24). Leaders with faith cause increase in the kingdom. Faith causes an entrance into the kingdom, and your faith can grow while living in the kingdom. In other words, we can and should grow in the kingdom (2 Thess. 1:3).

The righteousness of the kingdom comes by faith. We are justified by faith (Rom. 1:17). The kingdom would come through faith and not through the works of the Law. This was the issue in the early church. The Pharisees were depending on the works of the Law. The kingdom could not be entered by works. Abraham was justified by faith before the Law came. Many missed the kingdom because they tried to apprehend it through the works of the Law (Heb. 3:19).

Canaan was a picture, a type, of the kingdom. It was a land of promise, a land flowing with milk and honey. It was a land of prosperity, a type of rest. The generation in the wilderness could not enter in because of unbelief. Unbelief is what will keep you out of the kingdom. Faith will give you the ability to enter and enjoy the benefits of the kingdom.

The message of the kingdom came to a faithless and perverse generation (Matt. 17:17). This is why many in Israel did not receive it. They were walking in the same spirit as the generation in the wilderness. This had always been a problem. Notice this word through Isaiah:

> Again the LORD spoke to Ahaz, "Ask the LORD your
> God for a sign, whether in the deepest depths or in the

highest heights." But Ahaz said, "I will not ask; I will not put the LORD to the test." Then Isaiah said, "Hear now, you house of David! Is it not enough to try the patience of men? Will you try the patience of my God also? Therefore the Lord himself will give you a sign: The virgin will be with child and will give birth to a son, and will call him Immanuel."

—ISAIAH 7:10–14, NIV

Jesus was Emmanuel (Matt. 1:23). He was the sign given to an unbelieving generation. God was in their midst. The kingdom was in their midst.

THE EXPRESSION OF "HOSANNA"

There is significance in the expression "hosanna" and its relevance to the ushering in of the kingdom. Old Testament prophecy speaks about the appearance of the King when He enters Jerusalem:

Rejoice greatly, O Daughter of Zion! Shout, Daughter of Jerusalem! See, your king comes to you, righteous and having salvation, gentle and riding on a donkey, on a colt, the foal of a donkey.

—ZECHARIAH 9:9, NIV

This Old Testament prophecy was fulfilled when Jesus entered Jerusalem to the shouts of the people.

The next day the great crowd that had come for the Feast heard that Jesus was on his way to Jerusalem. They took palm branches and went out to meet him, shouting, "Hosanna!" "Blessed is he who comes in the name of the Lord!" "Blessed is the King of Israel!" Jesus found a young donkey and sat on it, as it is written:

"Do not be afraid, O Daughter of Zion; see, your king is coming, seated on a donkey's colt."

—JOHN 12:12–15, NIV

Jesus presented Himself as King by riding into the city riding upon a young donkey. Jesus came through the gates of the city. This is the picture of humility. Zechariah says He is "just," "having salvation," and "riding upon a donkey" (Zech. 9:9). Rulers commonly rode donkeys if they came in peace (Judg. 5:10; 10:4; 12:14; 2 Sam. 16:2; 1 Kings 1:33), but they rode horses into war.

There were some in Israel who recognized the King. They cried, "Hosanna." Salvation had arrived. It was not a physical salvation from the Romans. Jesus did not come on a chariot with an army. He came riding on a donkey. He came to bring eternal salvation to those who believed.

Hosanna means "save us, deliver us." The Greek word *hosanna* was derived from the combination of two Hebrew words: *yaw-shah*, which means "to save or deliver," and *naw*, meaning "pray." It's most literal translation is, "Save/deliver us, I/we pray."[1] As it is used in the New Testament, *hosanna* is an expression meaning, "Save, I (we) pray." This expression of "hosanna" can be seen in Psalm 118:25 and was commonly used in the Feast of Tabernacles. The expression was filled with messianic expectations of deliverance.

This same expression of "hosanna" was shouted by the crowds as Jesus entered the city. This was a cry for salvation that would come through the king.

Those who went ahead and those who followed shouted, "Hosanna!" "Blessed is he who comes in the name of the Lord!" "Blessed is the coming kingdom of our father David!" "Hosanna in the highest!"

—MARK 11:9–10, NIV

This was the fulfillment of Psalm 118:25.

Salvation would bring forth prosperity. The remnant would prosper through the Messiah. "Hosanna" came out of the mouths of babes. What an adequate picture of the kingdom. They recognized the kingdom of their father David. They blessed the King who came in the name of the Lord.

> Lift up your heads, O you gates;
>> be lifted up, you ancient doors,
>> that the King of glory may come in.
> Who is this King of glory?
>> The LORD strong and mighty,
>> the LORD mighty in battle.
> Lift up your heads, O you gates;
>> lift them up, you ancient doors,
>> that the King of glory may come in.
> Who is he, this King of glory?
>> The LORD Almighty—
>> he is the King of glory.
>
> —PSALM 24:7–10, NIV

This psalm is believed by many to celebrate the return of the ark into Jerusalem by King David. The bringing of the ark is a picture of Christ coming into Jerusalem. Jesus is the Lord of glory.

This is also a Messianic psalm that speaks of Christ entering through the gates of heavenly Jerusalem. The gates were opened for the King of glory to enter. Jesus is enthroned as King in Zion. He came through the everlasting doors of the everlasting city. He is the Lord of armies. This signifies His victories over His enemies. Jesus opens the way for us to enter the great city. It is also a picture of us opening our hearts to allow the King entry.

Matthew Henry's Commentary gives us additional insight about Psalm 24:

This psalm is concerning the kingdom of Jesus Christ,

I. His providential kingdom, by which he rules the world (v. 1, 2).

II. The kingdom of his grace, by which he rules in his church.
1. Concerning the subjects of that kingdom; their character (v. 4, 6), their charter (v. 5).
2. Concerning the King of that kingdom; and a summons to all to give him admission (v. 7–10). It is supposed that the psalm was penned upon occasion of David's bringing up the ark to the place prepared for it, and that the intention of it was to lead the people above the pomp of external ceremonies to a holy life and faith in Christ, of whom the ark was a type.[2]

The Pharisees were upset by what they heard as Jesus entered Jerusalem. They did not like what they were hearing. The kingdom had arrived, and they were displeased. This was not what they were looking for. Jesus was not their idea of the king.

> But when the chief priests and the teachers of the law saw the wonderful things he did and the children shouting in the temple courts, "Hosanna to the Son of David," they were indignant. "Do you hear what these children are saying?" they asked him. "Yes," replied Jesus, "have you never read, 'From the lips of children and infants you, Lord, have called forth your praise'?"
> —MATTHEW 21:15–16, NIV

By taking a close look at the prophetic significance of Psalm 118:19–29, we see a picture of the humiliation and exaltation of our

Lord Jesus, His sufferings, and the glory that would follow. Verse 19 begins with the righteous man suffering at the hands of them who hate him. The account the psalmist gives of his troubles is very applicable to Christ: many hated Him without a cause; and God chastened Him sorely, bruised Him, and put Him to grief, that by His stripes we might be healed.[3] The psalmist's enemies are a description of the enemies of Christ. His enemies surrounded Him, but they would be destroyed.

The gates would be opened to the righteous. The gates of Zion would be opened to the nations. The stone that the builders rejected would become the head, the cornerstone. The elders, scribes, and chief priests rejected Christ, but He would become the chief cornerstone. The church would be built upon Him. The day of salvation would arrive, and the righteous would rejoice.

The gates of the earthly Jerusalem were closed at night. The gates of ancient cities were closed at night for safety and protection. Isaiah, however, prophesies that the gates would never be shut, day or night.

> Your gates will always stand open, they will never be shut, day or night, so that men may bring you the wealth of the nations—their kings led in triumphal procession.
>
> —ISAIAH 60:11, NIV

The gospel will be constantly and unceasingly offered to people. The doors of the church shall at no time be closed. By day and by night, at all seasons and in all places, people may come and obtain salvation. None shall be excluded because the gates are closed to them. The gates of the kingdom are never to be shut. The gates of the New Jerusalem are described in Revelation 21:25 (NIV): "On no day will its gates ever be shut, for there will be no night there."

The gates are open. The kingdom is open. The highway to Zion is open. The fountain is open. The Spirit and bride say, "Come." The way has been open.

GIVING AND THE KINGDOM

Those who live in the kingdom can tap into the power of giving. The nations would come with offerings. Giving is a key to prosperity.

> Give, and it will be given to you. A good measure, pressed down, shaken together and running over, will be poured into your lap. For with the measure you use, it will be measured to you.
>
> —LUKE 6:38, NIV

When we come under the rule of the King, we come under the rule of Jehovah-Jireh, the Lord our Provider. The King provides prosperity for His kingdom's citizens. Poverty is a demon that can be cast out through the power of the kingdom and giving.

Those who give glory to the Lord also bring offerings. The nations would come and give to the God of Israel.

> Then you shall see and be radiant, and your heart shall thrill and tremble with joy [at the glorious deliverance] and be enlarged; because the abundant wealth of the [Dead] Sea shall be turned to you, unto you shall the nations come with their treasures.
>
> —ISAIAH 60:5, AMP

This giving would no longer be a central place in Jerusalem. We can give and support ministries ordained by God. We can and should support God's "sent ones." We should support ministries that are advancing the kingdom through preaching, teaching, and demonstration.

> Ascribe to the LORD the glory due his name; bring an
> offering and come into his courts.
>
> —PSALM 96:8, NIV

> In everything I did, I showed you that by this kind of
> hard work we must help the weak, remembering the
> words the Lord Jesus himself said: "It is more blessed to
> give than to receive."
>
> —ACTS 20:35, NIV

Through giving we support the weak. Giving is a manifestation of love and compassion. It is more blessed to give than to receive. We labor not only to have our needs met but also to give (Eph. 4:28). Giving is a sign of righteousness. The righteous man *gives* (Ps. 112:5).

The Gentiles were being taught the blessing of sowing and reaping. The kingdom of God operates on the law of sowing and reaping. The kingdom is full of grace, and this grace is seen through giving. God is able to make all grace abound toward us when we give.

Some of the greatest teaching on giving came with the arrival of the kingdom (2 Cor. 9:6–10). The giving of the Gentile churches to the Jewish believers in distress at Jerusalem was a sign of their obedience to the gospel.

> You will be made rich in every way so that you can be
> generous on every occasion, and through us your gen-
> erosity will result in thanksgiving to God. This service
> that you perform is not only supplying the needs of
> God's people but is also overflowing in many expres-
> sions of thanks to God. Because of the service by which
> you have proved yourselves, men will praise God for
> the obedience that accompanies your confession of the
> gospel of Christ, and for your generosity in sharing

with them and with everyone else. And in their prayers for you their hearts will go out to you, because of the surpassing grace God has given you. Thanks be to God for his indescribable gift!

—2 CORINTHIANS 9:11–15, NIV

Giving is a sign of the grace of God in you. Giving is a sign of the kingdom in you. Giving affects others in a powerful way.

We need to see giving from a kingdom perspective. We need to see giving from an eternal perspective. Giving can affect generations to come. Giving results in many coming to the Lord as we support ministers and missionaries. We share in the eternal rewards with those who preach as we support them financially.

Giving churches are kingdom churches. Giving believers are kingdom believers. Giving releases tremendous blessings to the giver and receiver. Both are blessed.

The kingdom of God is based on *giving*. God *gave* His only Son (Rom. 8:32). The Son *gave* His life. The Father and Son *gave* us the gift of the Holy Spirit. When Jesus ascended, He *gave* some apostles and some prophets, and some evangelists, and some teachers. The Holy Spirit *gives* us gifts.

Those who have received Christ should have a revelation of God's generosity. God spared not His own Son. We should not spare when it comes to giving. God's generosity to us results in our generosity to others.

There is no lack in the kingdom. God freely gives us all things. The kingdom is filled with abundance. The kingdom is filled with generosity. The King is generous, and His citizens are generous.

The Pharisees were covetous and could not enter the kingdom. They were controlled by mammon.

> "No servant can serve two masters. Either he will hate
> the one and love the other, or he will be devoted to the
> one and despise the other. You cannot serve both God
> and Money." The Pharisees, who loved money, heard all
> this and were sneering at Jesus.
>
> —LUKE 16:13–14, NIV

Giving is a sign that a person is free from the control of mammon. Christ is Lord in the kingdom, not mammon. When one submits to the lordship of Christ, mammon's power is broken, and giving becomes a lifestyle.

The Pharisees would not enter the kingdom, and they prevented others from entering. They closed the door in the face of those trying to enter. Jesus pronounced a woe upon them for preventing others from entering the kingdom. Judgment came on them, and they were removed from their position of authority.

> Woe to you, teachers of the law and Pharisees, you hyp-
> ocrites! You shut the kingdom of heaven in men's faces.
> You yourselves do not enter, nor will you let those enter
> who are trying to.
>
> —MATTHEW 23:13, NIV

The Pharisees used fear to control the people. People were threatened with being put out of the synagogue. They were threatened with excommunication (John 9:22). The problem was that there was no salvation in the synagogue. Salvation is only in Christ. The fear of excommunication paralyzed many.

Many of the Jews who believed in Christ had to make a decision. Accept Christ and be excommunicated or submit to the Sanhedrin and miss the kingdom.

ANGELIC ASSISTANCE IN
ADVANCING THE KINGDOM

There are many breakthroughs in cities, regions, and nations that happen because of angelic assistance and intervention. Angels brought deliverance to the apostles and released judgments upon the enemies of the kingdom. Angels are invisible agents that serve the invisible King and His citizens.

The apostles received angelic assistance to help them overcome resistance to the kingdom. Peter was delivered from prison and told to go and preach in the temple.

> They arrested the apostles and put them in the public jail. But during the night an angel of the Lord opened the doors of the jail and brought them out. "Go, stand in the temple courts," he said, "and tell the people the full message of this new life."
> —ACTS 5:18–20, NIV

An angel smote Herod, and the Word of God grew and multiplied as a result. Angels are involved in the advance of the kingdom of God.

Angels help in evangelism. An angel directed Philip to go to Gaza (Acts 8:26). He met an Ethiopian eunuch of great authority under Candace, queen of Ethiopia. The eunuch was saved and baptized. He returned to Ethiopia with the gospel. Ethiopia became one of the first nations to be Christianized.

An angel appeared to Cornelius in a vision. The angel directed him to find Peter to hear the gospel. This was the breakthrough into the Gentile world.

An angel assisted Paul in his ministry to the Gentiles. The angel encouraged him on his journey to Rome. Paul would eventually preach the gospel in Rome, the capital city of the empire.

But now I urge you to keep up your courage, because not one of you will be lost; only the ship will be destroyed. Last night an angel of the God whose I am and whom I serve stood beside me and said, "Do not be afraid, Paul. You must stand trial before Caesar; and God has graciously given you the lives of all who sail with you."

—ACTS 27:22–24, NIV

CHAPTER 12

ETERNAL HALLMARKS OF THE KINGDOM

P SALM 45 IS one of the most powerful Messianic psalms about the King and His kingdom. In Hebrews 1:8 (NIV), Paul quotes from this psalm by saying, "But about the Son he says, 'Your throne, O God, will last for ever and ever, and righteousness will be the scepter of your kingdom.'"

Psalm 45 is a *miniature Song of Songs* that describes the beauty of the King and the bride. The King is anointed above His brethren (v. 2). The King would ride prosperously through the earth (v. 4). The King would have a righteous scepter; His authority will be justice and righteousness (v. 6). The King would love righteousness and hate iniquity (v. 7).

The bride would also be a worshiper of the King. The daughter of Tyre would come with gifts, referring to the Gentiles' coming to the King. The people would come with gladness and rejoicing. The children of the King would be made princes (kings), and His name would be remembered from generation to generation.

This psalm shows the relationship between the King and His people. We enjoy His presence and fragrance (v. 8). The King desires our beauty. Our songs, praise, and worship are beautiful to Him. The King is beautiful, and He beautifies His people with salvation.

This is also a picture of the marriage of the King to His bride. This is a picture of a marriage festival, with female attendants or bridesmaids of the highest rank attending Him, while the queen, in rich apparel (v. 13), stands ready for the nuptial procession. The *King's daughter* is a term of dignity. It is a picture of the bride of Christ, the church, who is the daughter of the great King, God.

The King is known for His grace, majesty, righteousness, authority, beauty, fragrance, power, truth, and meekness. He will ride prosperously (conduct a successful war) throughout the earth (the expansion of His kingdom). His church would also be beautiful and worship Him with gifts. The King rides with His sword coming out of His mouth, which is the Word of God (Rev. 19:15). The sword of the Spirit, the Word of God, the gospel, is the weapon used to subdue the nations.

THE SCEPTER OF RIGHTEOUSNESS

Righteousness is the scepter of the kingdom. Righteousness is justice. God's justice came upon Israel and Jerusalem for mistreating and killing His ambassadors. The vengeance of God came as a result of the shedding of innocent blood. The arrival of the kingdom would be the arrival of justice.

> Therefore I am sending you prophets and wise men and teachers. Some of them you will kill and crucify; others you will flog in your synagogues and pursue

> from town to town. And so upon you will come all the
> righteous blood that has been shed on earth, from the
> blood of righteous Abel to the blood of Zechariah son
> of Berekiah, whom you murdered between the temple
> and the altar. I tell you the truth, all this will come
> upon this generation.
>
> —MATTHEW 23:34–36, NIV

The justice of God came on that generation. The King established His rule though judgment. The kingdom was at hand, and repentance was necessary. The kingdom was established with justice and judgment. The kingdom is a manifestation of the righteousness of the King.

The kingdom would come in the midst of Christ's enemies. His adversaries would be broken with a rod of strength.

Psalm 110 is a psalm about Christ sitting on the right hand of power. The high priest would see Him on the right hand of power coming in judgment on the clouds.

> "Yes, it is as you say," Jesus replied. "But I say to all of
> you: In the future you will see the Son of Man sitting
> at the right hand of the Mighty One and coming on the
> clouds of heaven."
>
> —MATTHEW 26:64, NIV

The religious leaders were the enemies (adversaries) of Christ. They would face His judgment and the rod of His strength. The rod would come out of Zion; the judgment would be from heaven.

Psalm 110 also talks about His priesthood. Christ would be a King-Priest after the order of Melchizedek. He would sit on the throne as a King in judgment and a Priest in mercy. The King would be David's Son and Lord.

THE KINGDOM IS ESTABLISHED WITH ZEAL

> Of the increase of his government and peace there will
> be no end. He will reign on David's throne and over
> his kingdom, establishing and upholding it with justice
> and righteousness from that time on and forever. The
> zeal of the LORD Almighty will accomplish this.
>
> —ISAIAH 9:7, NIV

The kingdom was established through zeal. *Zeal* is "ardor, jealousy, jealous disposition (of husband)." The King was jealous as a covenant Husband to Israel. His jealousy was stirred because of covenant unfaithfulness. His wrath was stirred, and His judgment came. He sent His ambassadors to warn Israel. The kingdom was at hand. Justice was at hand. Righteousness was at hand. Vengeance was at hand. The rule of God was being enforced.

Those who called upon the name of the Lord would be delivered. There was a remnant that was saved. They survived His judgment because they put their trust in the Lord. The survivors inherited Zion. Those who came into the church were saved. Those who persecuted the church were judged. The kingdom came in justice, judgment, and salvation.

> And everyone who calls on the name of the LORD will
> be saved; for on Mount Zion and in Jerusalem there
> will be deliverance, as the LORD has said, among the
> survivors whom the LORD calls.
>
> —JOEL 2:32, NIV

This was the judgment and salvation of the invisible King. The King had died and ascended to heaven. He sent the Roman armies from His position in heaven. Although He was not visibly present, that generation saw His judgment. His position as King was verified by His judgment.

In Deuteronomy 4:11, we read a prophecy about this destruction: "You came near and stood at the foot of the mountain while it blazed with fire to the very heavens, with black clouds and deep darkness" (NIV).

The high priest would see the Lord coming in the clouds of heaven. They who pierced Him would see Him coming in the clouds. The clouds represent judgment. Every eye would see Him coming in judgment (Isa. 19:1; Rev. 1:7).

The Lord would come upon a cloud in judgment as He did in history upon disobedient nations. Jerusalem had become like Sodom and Egypt (Rev. 11:8) and faced judgment.

Daniel saw the cloud coming in relation to the kingdom:

> In my vision at night I looked, and there before me was one like a son of man, coming with the clouds of heaven. He approached the Ancient of Days and was led into his presence. He was given authority, glory and sovereign power; all peoples, nations and men of every language worshiped him. His dominion is an everlasting dominion that will not pass away, and his kingdom is one that will never be destroyed.
>
> —DANIEL 7:13–14, NIV

The coming in judgment upon Jerusalem was an integral part of establishing the kingdom. Daniel saw the timing of the kingdom (in the days of the Roman kings) and saw the cloud coming (judgment).

It is important to note that salvation also came with judgment (Isa. 33:22). There is deliverance and salvation in Zion. The King is a Judge and a Savior. The message of the kingdom was one of salvation in the midst of judgment.

THE OUTPOURING OF THE SPIRIT

The outpouring of the Holy Spirit would also occur while judgment was pending. Those who called upon the Lord would be saved. Many did call upon the Lord and received the gift of the Holy Spirit. The church was birthed and formed with the establishment of the kingdom.

> And afterward, I will pour out my Spirit on all people. Your sons and daughters will prophesy, your old men will dream dreams, your young men will see visions. Even on my servants, both men and women, I will pour out my Spirit in those days. I will show wonders in the heavens and on the earth, blood and fire and billows of smoke. The sun will be turned to darkness and the moon to blood before the coming of the great and dreadful day of the LORD. And everyone who calls on the name of the LORD will be saved; for on Mount Zion and in Jerusalem there will be deliverance, as the LORD has said, among the survivors whom the LORD calls.
>
> —JOEL 2:28–32, NIV

The prophets spoke of the outpouring of the Holy Spirit in connection with the kingdom. (See Isaiah 44:2–4.) The Holy Spirit was initially poured out upon believing Israel and later upon the Gentiles. The kingdom age is an age of the Holy Spirit. Israel was awaiting this outpouring. It came on the Day of Pentecost.

Pentecost was another sign that the kingdom was arriving. This was the fulfillment of Joel's prophecy and is connected to the Day of the Lord. The Day of the Lord was a day of judgment. This judgment was arriving, and salvation was being offered. Those who accepted were baptized with the Holy Spirit. Kingdom living is Spirit-filled living.

Joel's prophecy of judgment is coupled with a prophecy of blessing.

> The sun and moon will be darkened, and the stars no longer shine. The LORD will roar from Zion and thunder from Jerusalem; the earth and the sky will tremble. But the LORD will be a refuge for his people, a stronghold for the people of Israel. "Then you will know that I, the LORD your God, dwell in Zion, my holy hill. Jerusalem will be holy; never again will foreigners invade her. In that day the mountains will drip new wine, and the hills will flow with milk; all the ravines of Judah will run with water. A fountain will flow out of the LORD's house and will water the valley of acacias."
>
> —JOEL 3:15–18, NIV

Joel describes the arrival of the kingdom with hyperbolic language. The sun and moon would be darkened. The stars would withdraw their shining. The heavens and earth would shake. This symbolizes the removal of the old covenant system.

In the midst of this judgment, the Lord would be the hope of His people. There was salvation in Zion. The New Jerusalem would be holy, and no strangers would pass through.

Joel then describes the blessing of the kingdom. The mountains would drop down new wine. The hills would flow with milk. The rivers of Judah (praise) would flow with waters. A fountain would come forth in the house of the Lord (the church). The valley of Shittim (a very dry place) would be watered.

Kingdom living is filled with wine, milk, and water. This is symbolic of the life filled with the Holy Spirit. This is symbolic of prosperity and blessing. This is new covenant living. This was the salvation that came in the midst of judgment.

Zion, the Place of
Worship and Glory

Zion was the place of the ark of the covenant. The ark of the covenant was where God dwelt, spoke from, and revealed His glory to His people. (See Exodus 25:22; Psalm 80:1; Leviticus 16:2.) King David placed the ark in a tabernacle on Mount Zion, which he built as a place of worship where God could dwelt in the midst of His people. (See 1 Chronicles 16:4–37 and Psalm 9:11.)

The kingdom of God would be a time when God would set His tabernacle in the midst of His people. He tells us, "My dwelling place will be with them; I will be their God, and they will be my people" (Ezek. 37:27, NIV). From His position in Zion, He promises, "I will bring them back to live in Jerusalem; they will be my people, and I will be faithful and righteous to them as their God" (Zech. 8:8, NIV).

Paul teaches us that we—believers who have accepted the King and His kingdom—are the temple of God today. He says:

> What agreement is there between the temple of God and idols? For we are the temple of the living God. As God has said: "I will live with them and walk among them, and I will be their God, and they will be my people."
>
> —2 Corinthians 6:16, NIV

The establishment of God's kingdom and of His eternal position in Zion was prophesied in Isaiah: "Look on Zion, the city of our festivals; your eyes will see Jerusalem, a peaceful abode, a tent that will not be moved; its stakes will never be pulled up, nor any of its ropes broken" (Isa. 33:20, NIV).

The apostle John confirmed God's place among His people as a result of his great prophetic revelation in the Book of Revelation:

And I heard a loud voice from the throne saying, "Now the dwelling of God is with men, and he will live with them. They will be his people, and God himself will be with them and be their God."

—REVELATION 21:3, NIV

THE INCREASE OF PEACE IN THE KINGDOM

The increase of the government of God is connected to the increase of peace (*shalom*). Those who live under the rule of Messiah live under peace.

Of the greatness of his government and peace there will be no end. He will reign on David's throne and over his kingdom, establishing and upholding it with justice and righteousness from that time on and forever. The zeal of the LORD Almighty will accomplish this.

—ISAIAH 9:7, NIV

Just as Israel lived in peace (*shalom*, prosperity) during the days of Solomon, the new-covenant believer lives in peace under Jesus the Messiah. David prayed prophetically for his son Solomon and for peace to be a hallmark of his reign: "In his days the righteous will flourish; prosperity will abound till the moon is no more. He will rule from sea to sea and from the River to the ends of the earth" (Ps. 72:7–8, NIV).

The dominion and peace of Solomon is a picture of the dominion and peace of Christ (Ps. 37:11). Jerusalem was to be a city of peace (Ps. 122:7). The Jews prayed for the peace of Jerusalem and still do. Jerusalem never experienced that peace outside of Solomon's reign.

Jesus spoke these words over the city:

> If you, even you, had only known on this day what
> would bring you peace—but now it is hidden from
> your eyes.
>
> —LUKE 19:42, NIV

Jerusalem missed her peace and missed her time of visitation. Instead of peace the city was judged and destroyed. The peace of God is now in the New Jerusalem, Zion, the new covenant city. Jerusalem would not experience the peace of God.

This covenant of peace (*shalom*) will be an everlasting covenant. God set His sanctuary among His people. God's sanctuary is His dwelling place, Zion. The old covenant sanctuary was a type of the New Testament sanctuary, the church. We are now God's temple, His sanctuary. This sanctuary began in Jerusalem on the Day of Pentecost. God set His sanctuary in the midst of Israel.

An important theme in the Book of Ezekiel is this: "You will know that I am the LORD" (Ezek. 16:62, NIV). Israel would know the Lord through the new covenant. Israel would know the Lord through judgment and salvation. The arrival of the kingdom would mean the arrival of the new covenant, the arrival of judgment (the Day of the Lord), and the arrival of salvation and redemption. This is why we need to understand the message, "Repent, for the kingdom of heaven is at hand," in its first-century context.

Israel would know the Lord through the new covenant.

> "No longer will a man teach his neighbor, or a man
> his brother, saying, 'Know the LORD,' because they will
> all know me, from the least of them to the greatest,"
> declares the LORD. "For I will forgive their wickedness
> and will remember their sins no more."
>
> —JEREMIAH 31:34, NIV

We know the Lord through the new covenant. The kingdom, the new covenant, salvation, and peace all converged and came together at the end of the old covenant age.

The peace of the kingdom would come through the sufferings and stripes of Jesus (Isa. 53:5). The result would also be healing. Israel would be healed of her backslidings through the new covenant.

THE KINGDOM BRINGS RESTORATION AND HEALING

The prophet Hosea married a harlot, representing Israel's harlotry in breaking covenant. Hosea saw the day when Israel would be healed of its harlotry and backsliding. This is a part of Hosea's vision of the kingdom. Healing would come through the suffering Messiah. The kingdom would come through Christ's suffering: "I will heal their waywardness and love them freely, for my anger has turned away from them" (Hos. 14:4, NIV).

The kingdom is a time of health, cure, and abundance of peace and truth (Jer. 33:6). This all comes through the work of Christ. This healing is also represented by the waters that flow from the temple in Jerusalem (Ezek. 47:8).

The sea and the waters represent the nations. Israel is healed, and the nations are healed. Israel was the first nation to experience salvation. The gospel then went to the Gentiles, who experienced salvation and healing, benefits of the new covenant, Zion, the New Jerusalem, the new temple, and the waters that flow from Zion and the temple.

Ezekiel gives us a picture of restoration:

> This land that was laid waste has become like the garden of Eden; the cities that were lying in ruins, desolate and destroyed, are now fortified and inhabited.
>
> —EZEKIEL 36:35, NIV

The cities were ruined because of judgment and captivity. Eden is a picture of dominion and communion with God. In the place of a curse and barrenness come blessing and fruitfulness.

THE KING IN HIS KINGDOM

THE REVELATION OF the King establishing His kingdom is powerful, inspiring, and life-transforming. As believers we are positioned with Him in His kingdom, and we have been instructed to spread the news of His kingdom wherever we go, that others may choose to be a part of His kingdom also.

Zion is the city of truth, the mountain of the Lord. The Lord has returned to heavenly Zion, and soon His kingdom will rule the world forever from the New Jerusalem. The King has announced His return to Zion and the establishment of His kingdom.

> Thus saith the LORD; I am returned unto Zion, and will dwell in the midst of Jerusalem: and Jerusalem shall be called a city of truth; and the mountain of the LORD of hosts the holy mountain.
>
> —ZECHARIAH 8:3, KJV

Zion is the city of truth, the mountain of the Lord of armies. *Truth* is the Hebrew word *emeth*, meaning "firmness, faithfulness, truth." Zion would be a faithful city, a city faithful to covenant. The unfaithfulness of earthly Zion will be replaced by the faithfulness of heavenly Zion (the church).

The kingdom would bring a revelation of Christ our Righteousness. Righteousness would not come through the Law but through Jesus Christ. This is the righteousness that is of faith. Jesus is the Lord our Righteousness, *Jehovah-Tsidkenu*.

> In those days, and at that time, will I cause the Branch of righteousness to grow up unto David; and he shall execute judgment and righteousness in the land. In those days shall Judah be saved, and Jerusalem shall dwell safely: and this is the name wherewith she shall be called, The LORD our righteousness.
>
> —JEREMIAH 33:15–16, KJV

Judgment and justice would be executed upon Israel, and salvation would come. This is a theme of the prophets—out of judgment would come salvation. The proud would be judged, but the meek would be delivered.

God brings judgment for the salvation of His people.

> You marched through the land in indignation; You trampled the nations in anger. You went forth for the salvation of Your people, for salvation with Your Anointed. You struck the head from the house of the wicked, by laying bare from foundation to neck.
>
> —HABAKKUK 3:12–13

This is what the prophet Habakkuk saw. God's purposes result in salvation. God judged Egypt for the salvation of His people and to make His power known to the nations. God's judgment would come upon the old covenant system, and His power would be made known to the nations.

> For the earth will be filled with the knowledge of the
> glory of the LORD, as the waters cover the sea.
> —HABAKKUK 2:14

Habakkuk saw the earth being filled with the knowledge of the glory of the Lord. This was God's ultimate purpose and would come through judgment.

THE EXCELLENCY OF CARMEL

> It shall blossom abundantly and rejoice, even with joy
> and singing. The glory of Lebanon shall be given to it,
> the excellence of Carmel and Sharon. They shall see the
> glory of the LORD, the excellency of our God.
> —ISAIAH 35:2

The kingdom is likened unto Carmel and Sharon. These are two places of beauty and abundance in ancient Israel. This is a picture of abundant life in the kingdom. It is a picture of salvation and restoration. It is a picture of joy and rejoicing. It is a picture of the glory of the kingdom. May your life blossom as a rose of Sharon through Christ. May you experience the abundance and beauty of Carmel through Christ.

The kingdom is the *excellency of Carmel*. In every passage of Scripture that mentions "excellency" or that which is excellent, the term carries with it a connotation of perfection, completion, and fullness. There is no lack in the kingdom. The kingdom has everything we need to live a happy and abundant life. The kingdom is perfect, complete, and full. There is perfection, completion, and fullness in Christ.

The sense here is that it shall blossom in abundance. The sense here is that the change would be as great under the blessings of the Messiah's reign as if the majesty and glory of Mount Lebanon should suddenly be transferred to the waste of the Judean wilderness. The excellence of Carmel was emblematic of beauty, as Lebanon was of majesty and as Sharon was of fertility. The blessings of the times of the Messiah would be as great, compared with what had existed before, as if the desert were made as lovely as Carmel and as fertile as Sharon. The world then—in regard to comfort, intelligence, and piety—might be compared to a pathless desert but would be like the beauty of Carmel and the fertility of Sharon.

I believe the teaching in this book will help you comprehend the greatest kingdom of all. Hopefully it will provoke the reader to study it further. There is no limit to this eternal kingdom. We have not exhausted the revelation of this important subject. We must continue to study and proclaim the truth of the kingdom of God.

The understanding of the kingdom will change your life and perspective. It will change the way you look at the future.

> Hope deferred makes the heart sick, but when the desire comes, it is a tree of life.
>
> —PROVERBS 13:12

The kingdom is a tree of life. Jesus, the King, is a tree of life. Eat from this tree and enjoy the abundant life of the kingdom.

There is no substitute for the kingdom. The kingdom is what Jesus came to establish, and it is our responsibility to advance it from generation to generation. Let us recommit and rededicate ourselves to the kingdom. Let us understand and teach it to the next generation. The truth of the kingdom must be recovered. Josiah recovered the

Law, and revival came to Israel. I believe the recovery of these truths will bring revival and glory for generations to come. I encourage the reader to review and meditate on the truths shared in this book. It has taken years of study to understand them, and it will take time to digest them. Review them and by all means share them through preaching and teaching.

Shalom.

NOTES

CHAPTER 1
A KINGDOM WITHOUT OBSERVATION

1. *Oxford English Dictionary*, third edition, online version, http://www
.oed.com, s.v. "perception."

2. Albert Barnes, *Barnes' Notes on the New Testament* (Kregel
Publications, 1962), s.v. "John 8:36," 351, http://books.google.com/
books?id=qvXCoSQ1yoEC&dq=Barnes (accessed January 10, 2011).

3. Matthew Henry, *Matthew Henry's Concise Commentary,* s.v. "John
18:33–34," ChristNotes.org, http://www.christnotes.org/commentary
.php?com=mhc&b=43&c=18 (accessed January 10, 2011).

4. Adam Clarke, *Adam Clarke's Commentary*, Electronic Database,
copyright © 1996 by Biblesoft, s.v. "Hebrews 12:22."

5. Henry, *Matthew Henry's Concise Commentary,* s.v. "Psalm 19:1–6,"
http://www.christnotes.org/commentary.php?com=mhc&b=19&c=19 (accessed
May 13, 2011),

6. Theopedia.com, s.v. "Imprecatory Psalms," http://www.theopedia
.com/Imprecatory_Psalms (accessed January 11, 2011).

7. Ibid.

CHAPTER 2
THE INVISIBLE KING

1. *Merriam-Webster Online Dictionary*, s.v. "invisible," http://www
.merriam-webster.com/dictionary/invisible (accessed March 16, 2011).

2. Ibid., s.v. "glory," http://www.merriam-webster.com/dictionary/glory
(accessed March 16, 2011).

3. Ibid., s.v. "splendor," http://www.merriam-webster.com/dictionary/
splendor (accessed March 16, 2011).

4. Ibid., s.v. "majesty," http://www.merriam-webster.com/dictionary/
majesty (accessed March 16, 2011).

CHAPTER 3
THE KING OF SAINTS

1. Barnes, *Barnes' Notes on the New Testament*, s.v. "Luke 17:20," 238.

2. Sir Lancelot C. L. Brenton, *The Septuagint With Apocrypha: English*
(London: Samuel Bagster & Sons, 1851), s.v. "Psalm 87:5," http://www.ecmarsh
.com/lxx/ (accessed January 10, 2011).

3. Barnes, *Barnes' Notes on the New Testament*, s.v. "Isaiah 66:8," From
Barnes' Notes, Electronic Database. Copyright © 1997 by Biblesoft.

4. Matthew Henry, *A Commentary Upon the Holy Bible, Isaiah to Mal-
achi* (London: Henry and Scott, 1834), s.v. "Isaiah 66:5–14," 168, http://books
.google.com/books?id=hnJAAAAAcAAJ&printsec=frontcover&source=gbs_
ge_summary_r&cad=0#v=onepage&q&f=false (accessed January 10, 2011).

CHAPTER 4
THE ROLE OF THE GOOD SHEPHERD

1. "Vocabulary," The National Heritage Museum online, http://
nationalheritagemuseum.typepad.com/learning/vocabulary.html (accessed
March 17, 2011).

2. *Theological Word Book of the Old Testament* (the King James Version Old Testament Lexicon), s.v. "Ra'ah, Strong's number 07462," http://
www.biblestudytools.com/lexicons/hebrew/kjv/raah-3.html (accessed March
17, 2011).

CHAPTER 5
THE CHARACTERISTICS OF THE KINGDOM

1. *Theological Dictionary of the New Testament* (the New American
Standard New Testament Greek Lexicon), s.v. "Soteria, Strong's number

4991," http://www.biblestudytools.com/lexicons/greek/nas/soteria.html (accessed March 17, 2011).

2. Adam Clarke, *Clarke's Commentary on the Bible*, s.v. "Luke 17:20," http://biblecommenter.com/luke/17-20.htm (accessed March 17, 2011).

3. David Guzik, "Isaiah 26—Judah's Kingdom of God Song," *Enduring Word Media*, http://www.enduringword.com/commentaries/2326.htm (accessed March 16, 2011).

CHAPTER 6
PROPHETIC VISIONS OF THE KINGDOM

1. Charles F. Pfeiffer and Everett F. Harrison, eds., *The Wycliffe Bible Commentary*, Electronic Database. Copyright © 1962 by Moody Press.

2. Ibid.

CHAPTER 7
MANIFESTO OF THE KINGDOM

1. *Merriam-Webster Online Dictionary*, s.v. "manifesto," http://www
.merriam-webster.com/dictionary/manifesto (accessed March 16, 2011).

2. Pfeiffer and Harrison, eds., *The Wycliffe Bible Commentary*.

CHAPTER 8
THE CHURCH AND THE KINGDOM

1. *Merriam-Webster Online Dictionary*, s.v. "ambassador," http://www
.merriam-webster.com/dictionary/ambassador (accessed March 16, 2011).

2. C. Peter Wagner, *Acts of the Holy Spirit* (Ventura, CA: Gospel Light, 2000), 49.

CHAPTER 9
GROWTH AND ADVANCEMENT OF THE KINGDOM

1. Alan Knox, "Continued Proclamation About the Kingdom of God in Acts," http://www.alanknox.net/2010/04/continued-proclamation-about-the
-kingdom-of-god-in-acts/ (accessed January 18, 2011).

2. Barnes, *Barnes' Notes on the New Testament*, s.v. "Acts 1:8."

3. John Gill, *John Gill's Exposition of the Entire Bible*, s.v. "Psalm 2:8," FreeGrace.net, http://www.freegrace.net/gill/ (accessed January 18, 2011).

4. Wagner, *Acts of the Holy Spirit*, 47.

5. Warren W. Wiersbe, *The Bible Exposition Commentary*, Vol. 1 (Elgin, IL: David C. Cook, 1996), s.v. "Acts 17:16."

6. Marv Nelson, "Cross-Cultural Missions," *See Through* (blog), http://youthmaster.blogspot.com/2010/11/cross-cultural-missions.html (accessed March 16, 2011).

7. Camille Paglia, cited from an America Online chat, 1995, "Western Culture," Jahsonic.com, http://www.jahsonic.com/WesternCulture.html (accessed January 18, 2011).

8. *Theological Dictionary of the New Testament*, s.v. "Porneia, Strong's number 4202," SearchGodsWord.org, http://www.searchgodsword.org/lex/grk/view.cgi?number=4202 (accessed March 16, 2010).

9. Doyle Lynch, "Being a Light in the Midst of a Crooked and Perverse Generation," DigtheBible.org, http://www.digbible.org/tour/bslight.html (accessed January 19, 2011).

CHAPTER 10
WOMEN AND THE KINGDOM

1. Frank Viola, "God's View of a Woman," Present Testimony Ministry, http://www.ptmin.org/view.htm (accessed March 16, 2011).

2. Solomon Ganzfried, trans. Hyman Goldin, *Code of Jewish Law,* vol. 4 (New York: Hebrew Publishing Company, 2004), 20.

3. Barnes, *Barnes' Notes on the New Testament,* 944.

4. F. F. Bruce, *The New Century Bible Commentary: 1 and 2 Corinthians* (New York: Harper Collins, 1981).

5. Dianne D. McDonnell, "Let the Women Keep Silent in the Churches—What Did Paul Mean?" The Church of God Dallas–Fort Worth, http://www.churchofgoddfw.com/monthly/Silent.html (accessed March 16, 2011).

6. Mimi Haddad, "Women Should Remain Silent?" *Sojourners,* http://blog.sojo.net/2009/04/02/women-should-remain-silent/ (accessed March 16, 2011).

CHAPTER 11
THE TOOLS OF ADVANCEMENT

1. Wayne Blank, "Hosanna," *The Church of God Daily Bible Study,* http://www.keyway.ca/htm2001/20010815.htm (accessed March 16, 2011).

2. Matthew Henry, *Matthew Henry's Commentary on the Whole Bible: New Modern Edition.* Electronic Database. Copyright © 1991 by Hendrickson Publishers, Inc., s.v. "Psalm 24."

3. Ibid.

MORE DYNAMIC TEACHING FROM APOSTLE JOHN ECKHARDT

If you enjoyed *The Invisible King and His Kingdom*, you will love...

GOD'S STRATEGY FOR THE APOSTOLIC AND THE BIBLICAL FOUNDATION FOR ITS USE AND PATTERNS

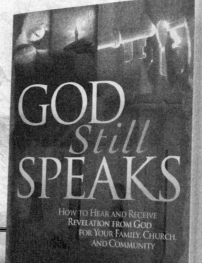

978-1-61638-166-0 / $14.99

ANYONE CAN HEAR THE VOICE OF GOD...INCLUDING YOU!

978-1-59979-475-4 / $14.99

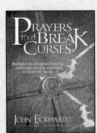

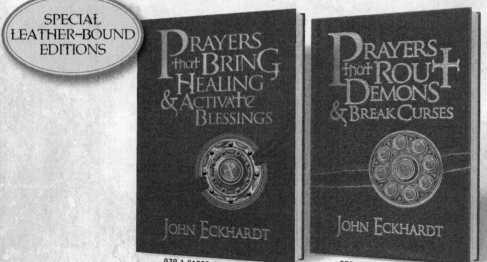